PERSONAL DEVELOPMENT IN COUNSELLOR TRAINING

COUNSELLOR TRAINER AND SUPERVISOR SERIES

PERSONAL DEVELOPMENT IN COUNSELLOR TRAINING

Hazel Johns

CASSELL

Cassell

Wellington House
125 Strand
London WC2R 0BB

127 West 24th Street
New York
NY 10011

First published 1996

British Library Cataloguing-in-Publication Data
A catalogue record for this book is available from the British Library.

ISBN 0-304-32935-5 (hardback)
0-304-32933-9 (paperback)

Typeset by York House Typographic Ltd, London
Printed and bound in Great Britain by Biddles Limited, Guildford and King's Lynn

Contents

TO THE MEMORY OF MY FATHER, TREVOR JOHNS

Foreword

I first trained as a counsellor in 1975. Since that time interest in counselling in Britain has mushroomed. For example, membership of the British Association for Counselling (BAC) continues to grow and training courses in counselling are cropping up everywhere. Fortunately, this growth in the development of counselling in Britain has been paralleled by an increasing concern that counsellors need to be properly trained and their work professionally supervised. The Counsellor Trainer and Supervisor series is designed to reflect this developing interest in the training and supervision of counsellors. It is the first series in Britain devoted to these two important and related professional activities and seeks to provide a forum for leading counsellor trainers and supervisors to share their experience with their novice and experienced colleagues.

This volume in the series considers how counsellor trainers might foster the personal development of trainees. Drawing on her vast experience as a counsellor trainer, Hazel Johns considers all the salient issues that pertain to this integrating core of such training. One of the strengths of Hazel Johns' book is that she adopts a broad perspective and considers how trainers from different orientations tackle the task of developing the trainee as a person. As such, this book will be of value to all counsellor trainers.

Windy Dryden

Preface

Personal development is not an event but a process, life-long and career-long: it must and will happen incidentally before and after any training course, through all aspects of life and work. I will argue that in counselling training it should be purposeful, integrated and at the heart of the learning journey of becoming a counsellor.

Counselling is a relatively young field at a fascinating and complex point of development. It is little more than thirty years since the first full-time training courses were introduced into Britain; we are currently in the middle of an explosion of training provision, full- and part-time, long and short, in-depth and introductory, in many settings, with a range of theoretical orientations and aimed at a variety of client groups. Counselling is also at a point of transition: increasing professionalization, the rapid growth of the British Association for Counselling and similar organizations, and new challenges such as the advent of National Vocational Qualifications, a Register of qualified practitioners and social and technological change as we approach the twenty-first century. Alongside such expansion, counselling training also faces constraint, as courses become longer and more intensive and fees higher. There is a tension between depth and quality of training and the dangers of elitism: duration and cost exclude many able potential counsellors and those wishing to be more proficient and ethical in the use of counselling skills.

As counselling becomes more accepted and less stigmatized, the *person* of the counsellor is seen as more significant than ever: hence, the importance of personal development in training at all levels. Much of what I say here is relevant also to psychotherapy training, trainers and trainees: since I cannot attempt, in the scale of this book, to engage in the debate about the sameness of or differences between them, I have stayed rigorously with the language of counselling. Since I am female and the majority of counselling trainees are also women, I have tended to use 'she' as the personal pronoun; the sprinkling throughout of 'he' demonstrates my affection for and acceptance of both genders as counsellors, clients, supervisors, trainees and trainers. Similarly, I respect and value the role of 'student'; some people find it a diminishing label, so I have, in general, used the term 'trainee' throughout. Trainees from whom I quote to illustrate direct experience have been disguised in identity, but are selected from real training contexts over many years and settings.

Inevitably, the more elements of training are engaged with the person and the personal, the more they are enmeshed with values and core attitudes. What I write here is as much what I have come to believe as what I know and think, coloured by my own history, training, commitment to fundamentally person-centred values and ways of working and influenced by personal experience of literature, music, art, being a client, counsellor, supervisor, trainer and human being.

My own personal and professional development has been influenced by many about whom I could write much, but this is not the place. I do want to thank by name those in particular without whom I would not have become the person and counsellor who has, at last, written a book!: Margaret Marshall, Douglas Hamblin, Francesca Inskipp, Jane Thomas, and, of course, from my beginning, my father, who was always proud of me, and my mother who is. I thank, too, Windy Dryden for his encouragement, and most of all, the colleagues, clients and trainees from whom I have learned so much.

I hope that trainees and trainers in counselling will find something here of interest and value.

Hazel Johns
January 1996

ONE

Who am I and who can I be for others?

What is personal development and why is it necessary?

BACKGROUND

I'm 39 and when I started the course, I thought I had life and me fairly well sorted-out. I have learned a lot this year about skills and clients and theories, but I've discovered far more than I expected about myself – and some of it has really surprised me!
(Extract from a trainee's personal statement at the end of Year One of a Diploma course in counselling)

That quotation highlights the sometimes unexpected significance of personal development for many people in counselling training. The desire for self-knowledge, the need for self-awareness and the hope of personal growth are hardly new or unique to counselling. Philosophers and writers throughout the ages have focused in prose and poetry on the essential mysteries of human nature. From Socrates in the fifth century B.C., with his great plea for self-exploration 'The unexamined life is not worth living' to Iris Murdoch (1983) 'We live in a fantasy world, a world of illusion. The great task in life is to find reality', they have been preoccupied with concepts of self and the meaning of life, self-understanding and insight, the pains, pleasures and confusions of interpersonal relationships and of individual life journeys.

In this century, in professional fields such as social work, management education and mental health, training has increasingly included work on self-awareness and self-discovery, the self in action, attitudes to others, values which inform, often implicitly, our behaviour and prejudices which distort our perceptions and responses. Even in medical training, for so long the bastion of supposed 'objectivity', and personal distance, attention is now being given to interpersonal skills, attitudes and values. A seminal

American textbook for teachers, with the significant title of *When Teachers Face Themselves* (Jersild,1955) centred around the questions 'Who and What and Why Am I?' and argued movingly that self-knowledge, self-awareness, self-understanding and, ultimately, self-acceptance are crucial for anyone helping others to manage those same tasks, as education – and, of course counselling – must be expected to do. Jersild points out the existential questions around the individual nature of meaning – the struggle to find the 'personal significance of everything we learn'; he also illuminates how much we know from developmental psychology of 'how great is the human capacity for self-repair'. Both those elements are central in personal development for counsellors, as are 'new consciousness and communication skills' in the task of 'deepening personal, professional and community relationships' explored by Miller *et al.* (1975) in work with families and couples. They argued that in American society (and certainly now in ours too) much of public life, advertising and commerce is exploitative and manipulative; people need compensatory opportunities and skills to improve the satisfaction from and integrity of relationships with others – again, key in counselling training.

In Britain, Annand (1977) argued for the centrality in education of personal development: 'A universal human incentive is the search for one's own nature and significance and place in things' and that the process of self-discovery is 'essentially social ... self-sufficiency is an illusion ... we become what we do become by interaction with others,' (Hemming, 1977). All these comments indicate key concepts which apply to personal development in general. Hemming also spoke eloquently of people's need for increased self-value and, with Satir (1978), for means of building self-esteem and confidence. In addition to this emphasis on the individual in interaction with others, there are two other facets of this work which have relevance for personal development in counselling training: firstly, that 'Those who help others to grow also grow' and secondly, that personal development in our culture has tended to emphasize the so-called 'feminine' qualities, synthesis, intuition, feelings and aesthetics. This has been in order to balance the traditionally valued 'masculine' elements of analysis, pragmatism, logic and order, which are constantly reinforced by formal education and most of the implicit messages of our culture. Hemming saw personal development as about the search for wholeness and, in particular, the search for and nourishing of neglected aspects of ourselves; both he and Morris (1977) argued for the need to value and develop our 'right brain' functions, creativity, imagination and sensitivity. Morris also acknowledged, though, that this meant 'discovering our powers of creativity, of construction and affection, but also our powers of destruction and hostility, and our capacity for fear', an aspect important for us as counsellors and trainers: the 'shadow' side of being human which as counsellors we have to work with in our clients and in ourselves.

If personal growth and awareness are so significant in education and in life, they are at least as important in counselling. In virtually all approaches to counselling, the relationship between counsellor and client is now generally accepted to be of central significance, if in a range of ways (McLeod, 1993). It must follow that 'Who Am I and Who Can I Be For Others?' are key questions: the counsellor has to accept that her 'self' is her principal tool/instrument. It is then unarguable that personal development – a consistent and continual striving for self and other awareness, knowledge, understanding and acceptance – should be an essential and indeed pre-eminent element in counselling training at any level, in any theoretical orientation and for any purpose or setting or client group. It is perhaps important to distinguish personal development from a more general personal growth, which the former will almost certainly encompass: personal development is a purposeful process, within the overall aim of professional development, in the service of clients and within the ethics and practice of counselling. As Dryden and Thorne (1991) stress – in something of an understatement – 'an unaware counsellor leading an unexamined life is likely to be a liability rather than an asset'.

MY PERSONAL DEVELOPMENT: WHO AM I?

As I struggle to write this book, it is inevitable that aspects of my own self and personal history, past and recent, are both helping and hindering me: what have I learned/not learned from my childhood and adult life; from nearly twenty-five years of being a counsellor, trainer and supervisor; what knowing/not knowing can I call upon to take me and the book forward? What indeed is 'personal development'?

I notice I want to say more about myself – since this is a book about personal development! – yet feel rather aghast at the thought that whatever I choose to say will be trapped as if in aspic on this page, for as long as the paper survives, and read by people to whom I cannot explain or reveal myself more fully or accurately. I realise, too, that that is a very significant part of my own development. I have chosen until now to define myself not as a writer but as a 'doer', in active face-to-face engagement with people with whom I can relate and debate in the moment. I must at the same time recognize how much family and cultural values have affected my responses to the visibility and exposure of writing – Welsh, first in my family to go to grammar school and university, hard-working, private, shy rather than extrovert. Paradoxically, I have spent my working life in quite public jobs, beginning as a teacher, now a counsellor–trainer, committed to openness, to being as transparent as I can dare or manage to be. Already, then, some key elements are emerging: me the person, my unique perceptions, thoughts, memories, feelings, attitudes, and values; my learning, knowing, awareness ... or lack of these ... and how to capture them; my own history ... or 'herstory' and its shadow or illumination on the present; my areas of confidence and competence or of limitations and anxieties; and, perhaps most of all, the range of paradoxes with which I shall have to struggle, both in the actual process of writing and, in some parallel ways, in personal development itself in counselling training. These seem to involve the desire for spontaneity yet the making of conscious choices, genuineness yet appropriateness of presentation, knowledge of the self yet acceptance of the unknown, movement and change yet stillness and focus, intimacy yet inevitable separateness, and, finally, efforts towards transparency, while acknowledging that we can only ever be partially visible, whether to ourselves or to other people.

'IF YOU DON'T KNOW WHERE YOU ARE GOING, YOU'LL PROBABLY END UP SOMEWHERE ELSE'

What does that phrase (the title of a 1974 popular self-help psychology book by Campbell) prompt you to think? Notice the ambiguities in the quotation: is it desirable always to know or helpful sometimes not to know?; is it helpful to reach a predictable destination or aim for an unknown one? The aphorism contains an essential paradox of personal development work in counselling training: it has been generally accepted that, as counsellors, we need to work towards self-awareness and self-knowledge; yet we must also strive for the willingness and confidence to take risks – of not always knowing, of not having certainties, of being able to be alongside ourselves and others in the mists of questions rather than answers. In my own life, my first response to the quotation above has generally been that it is important to work towards knowing, having a clear direction, that not knowing is somehow limiting, confusing and undesirable, if not dangerous. When, however, I allow myself more time to reflect on the statement, I can begin to feel the excitement of uncertainty, the willingness to take risks, to trust to a process, to trust myself and my ability to respond to whatever I meet. As Mitchell (1991) suggests, 'It is in being open and innocent that the possibility of understanding arises', while, inevitably, as in George Orwell's Room 101 in the novel *1984*, each of us will face different fears and different risks. Each counsellor in training is likely to uncover similar paradoxes which will need to be explored.

WHY PERSONAL DEVELOPMENT?

Personal development has been the least acknowledged and most intangible element of counselling training, yet, I will argue, it is the most essential. That, indeed, is the central theme of this book – that of the traditional trinity revered in adult learning – knowledge, skills and awareness – in counselling it is *awareness* – of self and others – which underpins *purposeful personal development* and it is these which should be seen as the cornerstone of counselling training. This is not to undermine the importance of theory and conceptual thinking about counselling, nor to diminish the attention given to solid and essential skills training – each sometimes undervalued in different training approaches and both contributing in many ways to personal development. It is rather to ensure that knowledge is more than sterile theory and skills are not merely mechanistic means to an end. I have already stressed the importance of an 'examined life' expressed in so many areas of our cultural inheritance: that, in order to have a full and satisfying existence, personal awareness and growth are core in any sensitive person's development. The key issue in terms of counselling training is the need to identify the particular ways in which personal development for counsellors is purposeful, specialized and more intensive. As Rogers (1961) expressed it: 'The degree to which I can create relationships which facilitate the growth of others as separate persons is a measure of the growth I have achieved in myself.'

WHAT IS INVOLVED IN PERSONAL DEVELOPMENT?

Imagine a new training group of eighteen to twenty people, mixed in age, background, gender, confidence and previous experience of counselling. What is their understanding of all this? I recently began a course with such a group; during the first day we undertook a 'brainstorming' exercise. The group was asked: 'As you begin this counselling training course, what does personal development mean to you?' These were their responses:

- Understanding myself better
- Finding my hang-ups
- Building skills with people
- Learning about my weaknesses
- Developing my strengths
- Growing-up!
- Finding what blocks my learning and my counselling
- Liking myself more
- Reaching my potential as a person and a counsellor
- Owning my good and bad selves
- Knowing what I want from other people and for myself
- Being not doing
- Past, present and future
- Being less self-conscious and more conscious
- Moving from anxiety to confidence
- Facing my fears
- Being angry and OK
- Realising my prejudices about others
- Becoming more aware

A comprehensive response which certainly indicated our curriculum for the next two years! What do some of these key words mean? Can we take for granted that we all understand them in the same way and make the same assumptions? What is this 'self' that counselling books (including this one!) keep alluding to? What does 'development' imply? How do we define 'growth' in this context? What is the significance of the emphasis on 'personal' as opposed to ... what? And if 'awareness' underpins all of these, what does it mean and is it possible to get hold of it? Why is all this so particularly important for 'counsellors'? I want to outline briefly what these terms mean to me, as I might at the start of any counselling course, in order to make visible my understanding of them.

The self

It has been said that 'the human organism seems capable of enduring anything in the universe except a clear, complete, fully conscious view of himself (*sic*) as he actually is' (Egan, 1973). Jourard (1964) reinforces this strongly: 'When a man does not acknowledge to himself who, what and how he is, he is out of touch with reality and he will sicken and die.' The premise here is that there is one way to define what the self means, while the reality is that there are many, depending on academic, philosophical, religious or theoretical approach.

Developmental psychologists and life-span theorists see human beings as 'becoming' throughout life, constantly changing in a changing environment. Maslow's (1970) 'self-actualising' person, Rogers' (1961) 'fully-functioning' person, and Erikson's (1980) eight-stage theory of psychosocial development, although all different in some dimensions, are some examples. (For a fuller description of these models see Sugarman, 1986). Existentialist philosophers and counsellors believe that people can make sense of life and of themselves by creating their own meaning; that we are essentially self-fulfilling and intrinsically flexible, within the acceptance that life has 'givens' and realistic limits, which we must face and within which we struggle to make the choices which shape our lives and ourselves (see van Deurzen-Smith, 1988). Winnicott (1971) promoted the relatively fixed concepts of true and false selves, while Assagioli (1975) in psychosynthesis defines both a personal self or 'I', seen as the centre of our consciousness, a point of pure self-awareness and will, and the transpersonal self, the 'point of pure, essential being which is unaffected by conscious experience' (see Whitmore, 1991). On a more earthly level, Wall (1977), described identity as 'an awareness of the self as distinct from the other, of a continuing, experiencing even though changing 'I' ... .' He emphasized, too, that we can more usefully be described as 'selves' rather than as a single entity or self and postulated that each of us must come to terms with ourselves as a physical person, a sexual person, a social person, a vocational person and a philosophical or 'moral' person. Rowan (1990), building on other frameworks including Freud, Jung, Assagioli, Berne, Goffman and Perls, also argues that we are more than a single personality or self, rather that we are composed of a number of sub-personalities. A co-tutor once described three, among others, of her sub-personalities as follows:

> *'Cookie' is the me who looks after people; she earns affection by nurturing, cooking lovely meals and taking real trouble to 'feed' others – she sometimes gets exhausted! 'Johnnie' is the outdoor me; she is happiest walking in the hills in casual gear, doesn't notice time passing, can be totally self-sufficient; she feels frustrated that she can't find enough time for herself and lets herself be neglected; 'Mary' often worries that work could take her over and that her sense of duty will be the death of her! On the other hand, that me sometimes seems the one most available, who can dominate all too easily … .*

In poetry, too, Robert Browning, among others, acknowledged a similar concept: 'Every person has two soul-sides, One to face the world with, and one to show a woman that he loves her'!

This movement away from a simple or simplistic understanding of the self is crucial, if we are to approach the whole concept of self and personal development with enough openness and flexibility. It is also important to remember that as individuals we almost never live our lives in a vacuum, but are constantly, as Oatley (1984) points out, engaged in a struggle for 'a right relation with ourselves and with others', so that the human being, the self, 'emerges from the interplay of community and individual experience'. Within that acceptance of our social and community existence, we must still recognise the uniqueness of the individual, the celebration of and respect for individual differences which underpin counselling and counselling training.

Development and growth

If, then, we can find a way of understanding what this 'self' is which we are supposed to be 'developing', what does that process involve? The starting point must be our common human experience that finding and maintaining an identity is difficult, when life involves an inevitable process of change and changes. These changes are of all sorts, large and small, predicted and unexpected, some chosen, some imposed, some in response to our unavoidable journey from birth to death, some in reaction to crises, some internal, others in the world around us, any moment every day, throughout life and as part of everyday living. A trainee recently recounted some of the changes she had identified during her first three months of counselling training:

> *My grandmother died – the last of that generation in the family; I've become a student again at 45; there are 27 'new' people (group members*

and tutors) in my mind and life – and I now 'belong' to a new institution; I've had my hair cut short after twenty years of having it long – a real change of image!; my weight has dropped; my husband suddenly feels quite jealous of and threatened by my separate interests; my daughter had an accident at school and we were called suddenly to the hospital; we're thinking of moving after being in this house since we married; my son brought his first girlfriend home from college; I think I'm starting the menopause ...

Our individual reactions to any one of those changes may be spontaneous and dependent on circumstances; involve automatic recourse to habitual learned patterns; and be affected by our wants, moods and responses of the moment. All, in turn, are influenced by our implicit attitudes, values, constructs, perceptions and needs, most of which we are unaware of and which are sometimes adaptive and effective and sometimes not. Gilmore (1973) quotes Bronowski's description of human beings as 'the repository of a unique set of experiences and ... thereby endowed with a unique set of choices.' Development, then, in the context of counselling training, necessitates bringing these responses, patterns and choices into awareness and involves some sense of purpose, directionality, continuity, planned activity in the direction of more effective living and working in counselling. The following example from a Diploma course member illustrates the kind of work which might be undertaken by someone who has begun to recognise a dysfunctional pattern of interpersonal interaction:

Goals for the next six months:

i) To record all the occasions when I feel hurt or not noticed;

ii) To explore in counselling and the small group what the triggers are;

iii) To try saying what I feel in the moment and at least check out the other person's intention;

iv) To monitor whether this has any spin-off with clients.

> (An entry in a learning journal, at the start of the second year, shared in a tutorial)

Carl Rogers (1961) highlighted this process of personal development as an essential element of 'the individual's efforts to become himself', while Mearns and Thorne (1988) comfortingly (and excitingly) remind us of the relationship between the counsellor-in-training and the human being engaged in the process: 'The counsellor's obligation to keep on growing is, in fact, a glorious invitation to live life to the full!' Growth, then, we might define as a product of all this – and as an end in itself – in which any individual's internal potential connects with the possibilities and opportunities available. These, together with the acquisition of the relevant skills and insights, enable the trainee to make the most of all those connections and apply them purposefully to her development as a person who is becoming a counsellor.

Personal and professional

Such research as is yet available (McLeod, 1993), seems to endorse the central concept that *who* counsels is more significant in terms of effectiveness than *what* is done and *how*. The importance then of giving due attention to personal development is unarguable. Increasingly in counselling training, a strong emphasis has been placed on the personal aspects of growth and development, in addition to, and in order to distinguish these from, what might more conventionally have been described as professional development. Although the history of counselling training in Britain (Bolger, 1982) demonstrates that there has always been an element of personal growth in all courses, the balance and extent has varied from course to course. In general, a range of parallel movements have coincided to ensure that increasing attention has been given to the personal aspect of counselling training: the burgeoning interest in personal choices and life opportunities since the Second World War (at least for many, though by no means all); the attention in education in the 1970s and 1980s to personal and social education in the secondary curriculum; the parallel attention to values and attitudes in health education; increasing focus on the individual in both popular psychology and journalistic writings; and, above all, the movement in the counselling field itself, in whatever theoretical orientation, towards an acceptance that the 'real' relationship between counsellor and client matters – whatever other techniques or concepts are going to be employed.

In counselling training, aspects of the personal on which we are likely to focus include:

- identifying and exploring the uniqueness and patterning of our values, attitudes and constructs;
- the elements in our personal family, relationship and educational history which facilitate or hinder our ability to feel, perceive, relate or protect/assert ourselves;
- the balance of our personal and interpersonal strengths and limitations;
- a sense of our emotional world, our capacity for intimacy with others and ability to stay separate and appropriately distanced from them;
- a knowledge of our needs, our fears, our intolerances;
- and, perhaps most significant, our passions and powers, our tendencies, inappropriately, to invade or deprive others.

We must also notice the inevitable interplay between our personal and professional selves: they may be separated for semantic or training purposes, but each, inextricably, contains the other. Professional development must focus, in parallel with personal exploration, on:

- the ethics and practice of counselling
- the needs of clients
- theory and skills
- supervision.

Central to all this must be the continuing struggle to communicate more effectively the 'core qualities' of *genuineness, acceptance* and *empathy* now regarded in every approach to counselling as the 'necessary' even if not the only elements in creating and maintaining a high-level helping relationship.

Awareness

Finally, then, we come to awareness – without which, furthering personal or professional development is impossible. What is it and how can we improve, heighten, increase our given quota? Is it, indeed, possible to extend any individual's ability? How, indeed, do individuals happen to have such apparently differing potential and capacity for awareness? It seems likely that individual differences in ability to perceive, register and note for use a range of cues in both the world around us and in our internal world have been reinforced or hindered by positive or painful experiences; differences in personality, motivation, interest, and capacity have combined with stimuli, opportunity and rewards to produce people with a very wide range of performance and with very different 'antennae'. Awareness seems to involve the ability to use all the five physical senses and to add to those whatever we might define as a 'sixth sense', that of intuition or however you conceptualize for yourself that phenomenon. All that then combines with the amazing ability of the human brain to process quickly a staggering volume of data, make choices and act appropriately – or not!

At the heart of all personal development work in counselling training, is the belief that people can increase their capacity for self and other awareness, and so extend their knowledge and understanding. This can then be put to the service of building a core counselling relationship for the benefit of any client, in which the counsellor's own emotional needs are not invested and human energy is creatively harnessed to positive effect. Counsellors are then more likely to be able to work within a clear and appropriate code of ethical practice, with insight, sensitivity and sound judgement, and, at the same time extend ability to work in truly non-discriminatory ways with a wide spectrum of clients and colleagues. We might also, as people, be more able to use emotions and social skills as currency for a healthy existence and coexistence with others: it is both fascinating and frustrating to observe the amount of energy, skill and resources poured into making us all technologically literate, while our cultural limitations in the awareness and expression of feelings – what we might call emotional liter-acy – are manifest in endless statistics concerning divorce, child abuse, neighbour conflicts, alienation and estrangement of all sorts.

VALUES

Carl Rogers (1978), exploring personal power, makes the 'common-sense' assertion that 'It is hopelessly idealistic to think that the human organism is basically trustworthy' – a paradoxical statement which he took delight in disproving throughout his life, work and writing. In some sense, much of what I believe – which underpins my understanding of personal develop-ment – could be dismissed as idealistic: people can grow; counselling train-ing is not a self-indulgent process, which benefits only a few; society could be a healthier context for more of us if we could learn to maximise some of the trustworthiness, strength and tenderness for which I see people having the potential; life is richer, if tougher, when we face rather than avoid diffi-culties; and if I know my gifts as well as my limitations, then I can make more fulfilling choices for myself, with others who matter to me and for society.

This book aims to explore, in counselling training in particular, the ways in which it is possible to move towards maturity, autonomy and interdepen-dent, appropriate relationships with others. Holmes and Lindley (1991) define autonomy as 'not extreme selfishness, nor a supposed independence from other people', rather, in its original meaning of 'self-government', control over one's own affairs. In other words, the aim is to work towards being able to gain insight into irrational beliefs and emotional disturbance; to understand the forces both outside and within ourselves; to be able to make choices, sustain emotional relationships in depth and develop the strength to do what we judge to be 'best'. I believe, with the philosopher John Stuart Mill (1806–73), discussed in depth in Holmes and Lindley (1991), that maturity includes the concepts both of pleasure and pain, that autonomy, in the sense outlined above, benefits both the individual and society. Holmes and Lindley argue for the importance of 'moral develop-ment': this they describe as leading to 'ethical sensitivity', including an awareness of our own 'fallibility' – if I can add *creativity* and *emotional literacy* to that, then it seems a useful enough framework for personal devel-opment.

If, then, we can 'face our selves' and work willingly for growth, self-understanding and self-acceptance in counselling training, we might be able to see, with Jersild (1955), that 'It is through my self – and through your self – that the intimacy of individual existence is realised, and it is also through this self that intimacy and relatedness with others is achieved. The self is the citadel of one's own being and worth and the stronghold from which one moves to others.'

SOME QUESTIONS

1. Are issues of personal development different in counselling than in other fields?

2. How might an 'unaware counsellor' be a liability?

3. What are your assumptions about the self? What is your 'image of the person'?

4. How do you see the relationship between the personal and the professional development of counsellors?

5. What do you see as your main focus at this stage of your own personal development?

6. What are your core values about counselling and being a counsellor?

TWO

In the eye of the beholder?

Personal development: Where does it happen and how does it vary?

COUNSELLING TRAINING: RANGE AND PURPOSES

Now, in the 1990's, counselling training encompasses a wide variety of courses, different in approach, settings, levels, theoretical frameworks and teaching and learning models. Courses in counselling exist for a range of purposes: to strengthen or improve the counselling part of a helping professional's multifaceted role (a social worker or personnel officer, for instance); to develop counselling skills in someone whose original training had a different emphasis, and whose function has changed (for example, a nurse who is specialising in cancer care); to introduce the concepts and skills of counselling to people for whom the process is new or misunderstood (perhaps the general public or managers in business and industry might be good illustrations); or to offer in-depth training to selected people who have made a commitment to become fully qualified counsellors. The levels of such courses – in detail, comprehensiveness, intensity and depth – will vary considerably, depending on purpose. Course balance and focus will be further influenced by underpinning theoretical or philosophical constructs, while contrasting teaching and learning models provide differing opportunities, both explicit and implicit, for processing all course material. Settings, too, in which courses take place will vary – from higher education institutions, to voluntary organizations to private companies; and counsellors-in-training will work with a wide range of clients.

Dryden (1991) has described counselling training as 'A delicate balance between self, skills and theory': that balance is unique in every course and training programme. The work on self and personal development will be similarly shaped and focused in a range of ways. The significance of personal development will be different in each course, yet it is always underpinned, I suggest, by some concepts and issues in common. In the first part of this chapter I shall attempt to highlight key commonalities, then in the second part of this and in the next chapter tease out some of the essential differences and their implications for personal development in course design in a range of approaches, levels and orientations of training.

COMMON ELEMENTS IN ALL COURSES

On any course, there are common key or core elements underpinning all work on self. Firstly, all the British Association for Counselling Codes of Ethics and Practice – for counsellors, counselling skills, supervisors and for trainers – emphasize the centrality of work on self, in order to become clear about, for instance, the appropriateness of attitudes, needs and emotions and the accuracy of perceptions. Secondly, in the interest of protecting clients, ethical standards are acknowledged, in all approaches and levels, to do with clarifying the boundaries between the worker and others, in order to avoid manipulation and oppression in counselling and similar helping relationships. These standards highlight especially the need to be discriminating about the appropriateness of feelings and behaviours, the relevance of roles and limits, the differences, for example, between social relationships, friendships, sexual relationships and counselling exchanges. For instance, the *Code of Ethics and Practice for Counsellors* emphasizes that:

> *A.1. Counselling is a non-exploitative activity. Its basic values are integrity, impartiality and respect ...*
>
> *B.2.2.5. Counsellors are responsible for setting and monitoring boundaries between the counselling relationship and any other kind of relationship, and making this explicit to the client.*
>
> *and 2.2.6. Counsellors must not exploit clients financially, sexually, emotionally, or in any other way ...*
>
> (BAC *Code of Ethics and Practice for Counsellors*, 1994)

All counselling training involves both a *task* – becoming a competent worker – and a *process* – a journey of personal learning for individuals. Embedded in that journey is the core need for increasing awareness of self and others. Similarly, again in any kind of counselling training, an almost inevitable process of change and transition is triggered for people, at the very least in the way individuals perceive others and in the range of ways that they are able to respond, as well as through insights and clearer perceptions into their own patterns and concerns. This is likely to happen for anyone open to any process of learning, which counselling training is on many levels. At the same time, the issues that stop people learning, that hinder the process and the journey can also come very clearly into awareness and be a very significant part of personal development: the 'blocks to learning' which may arise for a range of reasons and from many causes. At the end of any course, even a very short one day course, useful questions for participants can include:

- What have you learned about yourself?
- What have you learned about other people?
- What have you learned about the way you interact with people?
- What has stopped you learning today?

A member of a recent introductory course in counselling skills – her first contact with counselling training – responded vividly:

> *I've discovered that the part of me I thought I'd lost since giving up full-time work – the curious, confident, quite flirtatious, 'young' me – is very much around now – and other people like her! I am reminded that other people are at least as anxious as I am, even if they don't show it at first or hide behind status. That can make me feel put down and inadequate. N.B. One of the things that stopped me learning today is that I often censor what I say, so never find out if I am on the right track.*

Lots of potential personal learning there!

Perhaps the most substantial area of common ground is the underpinning theory that helps makes sense of personal development in a conceptual way. For example, aspects of social psychology, of developmental psychology and of systems theory are helpful in understanding the ways people respond, learn and change. Some examples from social psychology include self-image and the self-concept, ways of understanding personality, interpersonal attraction and prejudice, attitudes and perception; from developmental psychology, issues of age and stage, capacities for moral thoughts and emotional intimacy, maturity in all its forms and the relationship for any individual between her past and present. From systems theory, what seems important is the understanding that all human beings live in a context: they live within families, social settings, particular cultures, religious, ethnic, sexual and gender frameworks and they also live in the context of their own history and community, which inevitably affects their present existence. In some training courses, insufficient attention is given to making visible the significance of those theoretical frameworks; all those concepts are helpful, though they may be used in different ways and with different weighting. Certainly, trainers must have a sound grasp of all these issues and concepts, so that they can prompt course participants to ask questions of themselves and others. Such questioning might focus on the significance, among others, of any of the elements outlined here, in order to help clarify the core personal development questions of: Who am I? Who can I be for others?

Finally, in all training, in terms of personal development, I believe that a key element is the person of the trainer, the attitudes, values, understandings she models and the stimulus/energy she provides for all those processes at the heart of training. Chapter 6 will explore this aspect in more depth and highlight the significance of trainers' own personal development.

DIFFERENT COURSES: DIFFERENT PERSONAL DEVELOPMENT?

The previous section suggests some common elements in all courses; what are the significant differences amongst courses which affect the nature, extent, visibility, centrality and valuing of personal development work and which trainers need to bear in mind when designing courses? This section will explore some implications of the variations in courses of settings, contexts, levels and purpose.

SETTINGS

Counselling and counselling skills occur in many arenas, with a variety of client groups, on a range of issues and concerns and in many physical and organizational contexts. Similarly, counselling training is housed in a number of settings and backgrounds; these have significance for the particular status of personal development within any course. It is interesting always to question implicit influences on course design and the hidden agendas promoted in different settings and organizations. The three major settings in which counselling training currently occurs – voluntary organizations, higher education institutions and private or commercial firms – will vary in the balance of provision of personal development.

Higher education

In higher education contexts, the traditions of formal examinations, didactic teaching methods and intellectual emphasis were all still strong in the 1960s when counselling training began in Britain. The value of experiential and practice-based learning and personal development tended to be much underrated (Bolger, 1982). A hierarchy of values, implicit if not explicit, with facts, knowledge, objectivity and conceptual processes at their head, created a tension in course design for counselling in such settings. In order not to be regarded as 'newfangled', 'soft', 'mickey mouse' or 'unsound' (all terms I have heard used perjoratively) the temptation was considerable in the early days of course development to overemphasize theory and formal processes in order to ease course approval and earn acceptance on the system's own terms. In addition, many of the trainers on early counselling courses were not counsellors, but were academics, psychologists, social workers or from other related helping professions. It has taken time, persistence and much energy from individual trainers for counselling courses to be valued in their own right, with due weight for affect as well as intellect, for feeling and being to be seen as significant as thinking and doing, and for work on self in a range of ways to be accepted as legitimate and indeed essential.

In many such institutions, informal resistance from academic colleagues in this 'clash of cultures' has included personal hostility to and apparent fear of such work, together with internal competitive wrangling and power play about resources. Skills and competencies have gradually become accepted as part of academic courses, certainly those with a vocational focus. Personal development work, though, has at worst been dismissed as irrelevant and at best often been misunderstood; trainers sometimes in the past relied on imported training methods from North America, such as particular kinds of group work (see Chapter 9) or on models of development from other helping professions such as social work. At times, too, 'lip service' was often paid to the significance of work on self, while in reality such work was often tagged onto the course structure and lacked any sense of connection, integration or coherence. Since assessment was often very formal and theoretical study most highly regarded, any such non-assessed, non-integrated element of a counselling course could only be regarded with tension or ambivalence by students and engaged in with minimal commitment by some.

I have used the past tense so far in this section, since counselling courses in higher education institutions have benefited from the battles of the past and are generally regarded now as acceptable and even respectable! Gradual changes in other disciplines in teaching, learning and assessment methods have all contributed to the beginnings of a general shift in attitudes, with the design, emphasis and learning strategies of some counselling courses actually seen as modelling good practice for courses in other fields to follow: a satisfying reversal. Similarly, as subjective experience has become more valued, slowly in research methodology and even in 'new' science, the primacy of personal experience and the person of the learner are becoming increasingly accepted in many disciplines. Just as the therapeutic relationship has been acknowledged as central in the counselling process, so personal development in counselling training is gradually being viewed as core, integrated and the very vehicle through which theory and practice can and should be connected. As Connor (1994) outlines, 'all aspects of the training model are designed to feed into the sort of intra-personal and inter-personal development that will make a difference to the ability to form and sustain therapeutic relationships ... '. Given this redressing of the central place of personal development, higher education can be an excellent setting for counselling training: there is an expectation of a high standard of conceptual thinking and the capacity to evaluate and research, which courses in other contexts have traditionally perhaps underemphasized. Since, with Brigid Proctor (1978), I believe that 'every counsellor needs a theory' – indeed theories – to make sense of all that we do, the provision of an integrated, interconnected, rigorous learning process interweaving personal work, practical skills and theory is the soundest basis for counselling and counselling skills training. This potential for quality training provision is being further strengthened in, for instance, some universities. They have traditionally placed highest value on their own assessment and qualifications, but are now also willing to undertake the demands of the BAC course recognition process.

Voluntary Organizations

If higher education institutions have traditionally emphasized theory at the expense of other facets of training, then many voluntary organizations fall into different traps. Some, especially in earlier historical stages of counselling training, have seen personal development as the principal focus and purpose of their training programme, paid little attention to skills development and even less to conceptual frameworks. Early marriage guidance training, for instance, emphasized very strongly personal and interpersonal processes; a great deal of time was spent in groups exploring exhaustively intra- and interpersonal issues, with relatively little attention to skills and theory. That balance has more recently been markedly modified. Some training for bereavement counselling has a great emphasis on dealing first, and at length, with the counsellor's personal experiences of death and loss, to identify unfinished business or trigger points and to enable counsellors to tolerate the difficult or negative aspects of grief. This is a reasonable enough focus, but it should sit alongside relevant knowledge, such as 'bodily changes in dying and bereavement' (Stedeford, 1989) and a range of skills and techniques appropriately adapted which are also recognized as valuable. In contrast, some organizations dealing with particular client groups have focused training on counsellor acquisition of skills and knowledge and neglected personal work; some training in the drug and alcohol counselling field has had this bias. For example, Velleman (1989) suggested in a discussion on specialist or generic training that the creation of the Regional Drugs Training Unit 'greatly helped ... the transmission of knowledge and skills relating to drug use': reference to personal development was noticeably absent.

The key question, whatever voluntary organization, client group or training model is involved, is one of *balance*, appropriate proportioning of self, skills and theory work according to the needs of the client group concerned and the counsellors who are being trained. Many counsellors with voluntary agencies are, by definition, themselves volunteers, perhaps with fewer of the checks and balances (though not necessarily so) which the hurdles of formal education, selection, professional training and supervision may have provided. Personal work, then, should be absolutely central in training, particularly in terms of the exploration of motivation, values, prejudices and ethical safeguards. A central ethical concern is that counsellors should not be meeting their own emotional needs through their relationships with clients. Work on self-awareness and self-exploration is essential in training and throughout supervised practice in future development, but it needs to be related to appropriate theoretical concepts and applied and tested both in practical skills training and in actual work with clients. The part that supervision plays in the process may be very important indeed, especially in voluntary organizations where training resources are limited.

Commercial/private organizations

Counselling training run by independent organizations has proliferated in recent years, often providing courses in areas where none existed. A wider range, geographically and academically, of trainees have consequently had access to and opportunities for training. Courses in counselling run in these contexts are affected, perhaps more than others, by one major factor: they have to be at least economically viable and almost invariably need to make money, in order that the organization survives. Courses in higher education are often subsidized, if not in direct costs then in terms of buildings and some staffing resources; voluntary organizations have (or had) grants or charitable status: private training organizations must succeed financially. This may create problems; as Dryden and Feltham (1994) stress: 'courses which are primarily set up to make money and not to nurture, respect and assist students, to become professionally competent, do an obvious disservice' and 'predominantly independent commercial courses may be required to charge high fees and to hold large classes in order to survive or prosper economically'. Counselling training in general is staff intensive; personal development work, in particular, demands considerable resources of time, personnel and space in order to offer adequate, consistent and developmental support and challenge throughout the life of courses, especially long courses. This poses, I believe, a challenge to some commercial organizations, whose advertising in some cases may indicate the emphasis of their courses and cause some concern. Where counselling courses are predominantly theory or knowledge based; where course outcomes appear to hold promise of mastery of skills or techniques unconnected with other aspects of training; where there is no reference to personal development or work on self, then potential course members should look warily at the 'training product' (*sic*) on offer. The staffing of such courses may offer crucial clues to the organization's attitudes: BAC course recognition guidelines recommend a minimum staff student ratio of 1:12 where practical and personal work is undertaken at diploma or equivalent level. Others (Dryden and Thorne, 1991) advocate one staff member for every eight or ten students and state categorically that no course should be run by only one person. These views have been challenged by some commercial training organizations as inappropriate and a debate over minimum/optimum staffing is still under way. If the nature of the training task is considered (at any level but certainly for longer, in-depth courses) – sensitivities, range of goals, academic, practical and personal, interpersonal pressures, possible individual disturbance, complexity of group process, wide and deep curriculum, professional and ethical responsibilities – then pressures on trainers and trainees are clearly enormous and the process must be accepted as a highly demanding one. The particularly staff intensive elements of much personal development work, then, may be in danger of being reduced or even squeezed out in courses run by commercial organizations. Financial pressures, increasing group sizes and the demand to reduce costs currently affect all training organizations whether higher education, voluntary sector, or the commercial world; the wind can only be keener in a profit-making context and that elusive balance of self, skills and theory harder still to achieve. It should be stressed, of course, that courses in all contexts vary enormously in quality; some counselling training in the private sector is of at least as high a standard as some in higher education or the voluntary sector is poor. One difference, though, may be that the quality assurance procedures – the checks and balances from within and outside the organization – may be greater outside the private sector than within it, as audit and evaluation take a higher profile in organizations which have public money. The monitoring role of BAC is, of course, crucial here, as it acquires a higher profile as a professional 'watchdog'.

A further contentious issue in commercial provision is the potential for personal development in correspondence courses in counselling: some work is possible, appropriately focused through exercises, but the limits of such provision have to be faced. Lack of direct one-to-one and group experience will reduce significantly the nature and degree of personal development. There is some tension here between my own desire to make counselling training less exclusive and elitist, either in terms of cost or accessibility, and ethical questions of the essential elements and quality of such courses.

LEVELS AND PURPOSES OF TRAINING

When a trainer is designing a course, at whatever level and for whatever purpose, questions must constantly be asked about *balance*:

- What balance of time is to be given to the different elements?
- What attention at which stage to content and process?
- What is foreground and background at every stage of the course?
- What must be discrete and separated out and what should be integrated and implicit throughout?
- What must be both?

These questions are important for every aspect of the accepted learning trilogy of knowledge, skills and awareness, translated in a counselling context into theory, practice and work on self. Such questions need to be asked particularly for work on self, since it is often deemed to be more intangible, less easy to define, plan or structure. If I take, for illustration, three levels of counselling training courses, driven by three different aims, I can identify some significant differences in the what, how, why and when of personal development work and of legitimate trainer expectations.

Introductory courses for counselling or counselling skills

These, sometimes described as 'short' courses, can vary from a one day workshop to two or three hour sessions over twenty weeks. They share, usually, the features of no prior selection and a wide range in group membership in terms of age, social background and occupations. Motivation also varies from general interest, improving understanding of or performance in relationships, or as the first tentative steps to becoming a trained counsellor. Such courses generally offer some brief, simplified theoretical frameworks to stimulate understanding of what counselling is and is not; perhaps some basic practice in listening and core reflecting/paraphrasing skills – 'active listening'; and the beginnings of work on awareness of self and others. In some organizations in such courses, the last area – work on self – is missing, deemed impossible or inappropriate to manage in such a brief, relatively superficial course. This seems ethically and professionally unsound; at the very least, it is essential to flag the centrality of personal development in counselling training at any level and to allow course members to taste or feel some embryonic experience of it .There is otherwise a danger of offering only 'a mechanistic approach to counselling training' (Connor, 1994), so producing merely 'skilled technicians'.

Introducing course members to the concept of personal development can be effectively managed even on a one day workshop in at least three ways. Firstly the *content* or input of the course is likely to emphasize the importance of relationship in any attempt at a definition of counselling, so encouraging participants to reflect on their understanding to date. The core qualities of empathy, genuineness, and acceptance, together with the ability to communicate them, will be explored by individuals, perhaps naming them for the first time and linking them with their own ways of communicating. Some time will also be spent on blocks to giving attention and to listening, which will inevitably begin to focus participants on some of their own anxieties or preoccupations. These are some of the simple frameworks offered on even a very short introductory course, yet they immediately focus course members on aspects of themselves, their own personality, their styles of communicating and of making relationships, and the significance of all those for engaging in any way with the use of counselling and counselling skills.

Secondly, the kind of *practical exercises* chosen, however simple and basic, will highlight again the importance of the self, the person any trainee brings, to any level of counselling process. So, for example, in listening skills exercises, inviting people to share brief aspects of their own lives and experiences can perform effectively the triple functions of skills-learning, self-sharing and reflection (see further examples in Chapter 8). On the first morning of a three day introduction to counselling skills course, I might ask participants to work in pairs for twenty minutes, taking ten minutes each to listen, while the partner explores a difficult decision she is facing at present.

In the perennial training debate about the relative value of role play or real life experience, I unequivocally favour the latter: there is a place for role play in, for example, case study or developing empathy exercises or in the service of other training aims at more sophisticated levels, but where core learning is demanded about skills, qualities, attitudes and basic counselling processes, 'real' material is essential – and its use underscores the significance of personal development throughout all aspects of counselling training. As Dryden and Thorne (1991) stress, even in skills training, adequate support in cases of trainee distress and sensitive management in the training context are vital. Given such support and management in an appropriate 'holding environment', the gains are great. The counsellor can obtain from the recipient of the counselling, reliable feedback 'concerning the impact of the skill under consideration', while for the client some minimal experience of sharing real feelings in a client role can be invaluable at introductory level.

The other challenge offered by the use of trainees' own material is to any possible 'grandiosity of the helper'; to any delusion that counsellors or helpers are intrinsically different or better than clients, without issues or concerns to explore and feelings to face and untangle. That is perhaps an essential first step in any would-be counsellor's personal development!

Thirdly, even in the shortest of introductory courses, the *climate* of the course is crucial; as is how that is created and maintained by the tutor. If a receptive and open style is modelled by the tutor, course members are welcomed with some warmth, interaction is encouraged in the group in a safe and appropriate way throughout the day or session, then facilitative ground rules can emerge. Such a framework allows a willingness to make intrapersonal and interpersonal-process visible and expressed, however simply. This is a key aspect of any trainee's engagement with work on self. The trainer can encourage course members to notice, for example, what feelings they experience when asked to 'find a partner' for a skills exercise; what anxieties/expectations they are aware of in contemplating the work of the day or session; what range of responses they notice to other people in the group; and what they find easy to own to themselves or to talk about with others, in contrast to what self-censoring they find themselves doing. At the same time, the interplay may become apparent in individuals of past and present experiences, episodes of, for example, personal learning history triggered by responses in the training situation or echoes awakened of significant people in an individual's past, prompted by interaction with another group member. During a recent counselling skills course, a course member wrote the following in his summary of personal learning at the end of the first day and was then able to share it with his partner:

> *When I first saw Peter, I felt really uncomfortable – and I couldn't think why. When we worked together in the second pair exercise, I noticed that I was avoiding looking him in the eye. Then I realised that the particular set of his jaw was just like my brother's when we were kids and he was about to get me into trouble – which happened a lot! I could see Peter more clearly after that.*

By modelling some self-sharing at an appropriate tentative level, and even just by articulating relevant questions, the trainer can enable course members to begin to develop more awareness of feelings, sensations, prejudices, and blind spots, whether they share them verbally or not – and such awareness is the absolute keystone of any future personal development work. All of this can be worked with, especially by a skilled and sensitive trainer, using language of an appropriate level of technicality, avoiding jargon or theoretical concepts such as transference and attribution – though these can be introduced if this is relevant for the group and its learning needs.

Even at the most basic level of training there are considerable possibilities for personal development work, especially the heightening of self-awareness, Questions of balance – of time, attention, between theory, practice and work on self – and foreground/background focus must be borne in mind by trainers, as in any course at whatever level. Indeed, the trainer skills of running short, introductory courses are extensive, involving often subtle choices and the ability to discriminate. Trainers need to be able to judge pace, timing, level, language appropriateness and needs for support; to demonstrate active listening, immediacy and self-disclosure skills in modelling the communication of self-awareness; and perhaps particularly to use techniques for closing down as well as opening up expression, in order to maintain safe yet appropriate learning opportunities for what will be a wide-ranging group membership. This is a far cry from the fallacious (though often found) notion that introductory courses can be led by minimally experienced tutors! This may be true if only content is presented, is hard to sustain when the complexities of skills teaching and feedback are considered, and becomes a mockery of training when the sensitivities, self and other insights and carefully tuned antennae needed for this primary level of personal development work are fully in focus.

Certificate courses in counselling skills

Courses aimed at this level will have a mixed membership: they will include people undertaking some substantial early training which may lead them later to train as counsellors, some in helping relationships such as teachers, nurses, doctors, managers who want to improve their counselling skills as part of a broader function and some who see counselling skills as a way of improving communication and responsiveness in their own interpersonal relationships and activities. All are making quite a commitment to a one or two year course, and a deeper level of conceptual, practical and personal training. All the previous comments about the content, exercises and awareness work of short, introductory courses apply again in this context. In addition, more complex theoretical frameworks will be introduced, skills exercises can be used demanding more risk, especially deeper empathy and challenging skills, and more attention is likely to be given specifically to personal development in one-to-one work, through personal reflection and through experience over time in a group. At this level of training much of the work on self will still be implicit and indirect, triggered again by many parts of the course. Theory may be a vehicle for stimulating personal questioning; aspects, for example, of social psychology, such as interpersonal perception, communication and language issues or the introduction of role and self theories, may all provide fruitful filters to consider the person/ style/patterns of the course member. The likely emphasis on feedback skills in practical work, linked with intensive work on the more complex, challenging and self-disclosure skills will inevitably provoke self-exploration and increasing self-awareness.

The most significant differences, in terms of personal development in training of this kind, will be through the experience of overt interpersonal exchanges in a working group and from the processes of assessment. In my experience, assessment triggers some quite dramatic aspects of personal awareness and growth. In an award-bearing course like this, facing the pressures of self-assessment – almost unavoidable in counselling training – and tutor assessment often restimulates earlier learning anxieties, unfinished business with teachers and assessors from other life and learning stages and taps into performance, achievement or failure 'drivers' which had previously been unsurfaced. The pain of such internal messages such as 'I can only fail', or 'I'll never be good enough' or 'However hard I try I'll never make it' can be very shaking for adult learners; this pressure can be intensified if peer assessment is also an integral part of the course process. Making judgements and giving feedback openly and concretely and receiving feedback willingly and as non-defensively as possible can produce feelings of vulnerability, exposure, unexpected competitiveness, envy and negativity. Significant choices can be made by trainers concerning the amount of time and energy given in the course, especially in the large group or smaller subgroups, to processing such material and helping individuals identify useful personal learning from it. The course evaluation sheets from one of our certificate courses contained the following comments on assessment:

> *I didn't know what an ordeal the first video peer feedback session would be. I felt about fourteen and all the memories of team games at school came flooding back.*

'Not being good enough' is my theme – I felt we all became stuck in neg-
ative, critical mode. It was helpful to hear the others say they felt much the
same – perhaps we could have spent more time beforehand preparing for
the process? Nothing would have made it easy though.

Being in a working group, with an appropriate climate conducive to
exploration, is often a new opportunity for personal development, as is
encouragement to reflect on such learning in tutorials or through a personal journal, again found in many certificate level courses. (Further discussion of journals and tutorials as vehicles for personal development will
be found in Chapter 7.) Many course members also have the experience of
being for the first time in the relative intimacy of such a group for a substantial period (see Chapter 9). The accompanying informal contact in
breaks and between sessions will also involve degrees of bonding and raise
issues of personal attraction and antipathy, subgroupings and exclusions,
which may have much relevance for personal development, in particular,
triggering the exploration of reactions parallel to those which arise with
clients and colleagues. Differently than in short courses or in Diploma/
Masters level courses with their emphasis on professional development and
a range of counsellor goals, certificate course members often share a very
core feeling – that 'being there' is an end in itself. If 'bonds, goals and tasks'
(Dryden, 1992) are significant in training, then the personal issues and
awarenesses prompted by such contacts and shared purpose are often profound. As a consequence, students are likely to develop increased interest in
self-exploration for both personal and vocational purposes. Other useful
outcomes of certificate level training are likely to include the ability to discriminate amongst a range of skills or responses, depending on the role or
function that someone is in at the time and the needs/emotional state of the
person or other people; the potential to read cues from others more sensitively and understand the impact of interpersonal behaviours; and the
capacity to articulate and own personal feelings, needs and difficulties. All
this is in order to communicate more effectively, especially the 'core qualities', in creating any worthwhile interpersonal relationship. Of particular
significance, too, in courses at this level and with this focus, are the beginnings of integration of theory, skills and both implicit and explicit work on
self, together with some sense of their interdependence. I have real concerns about courses which, even in their titles, separate theory and skills
and make no mention at all of personal development. There are equally
grave concerns about courses – or tutors – who create an overemphasis on
personal work, with insufficient attention to skills and conceptual frameworks, so seducing students covertly into therapeutic growth groups for
which they may not be ready, prepared or supported. As always, in course
design and focus, purpose and balance are key questions.

Diploma and Masters courses

Counselling training at this level, particularly when courses have also earned BAC course recognition status (see Dryden *et al.*, 1995), will contain theory, skills and personal development work at a yet more sophisticated depth and, ideally, integration. These courses profess to train counsellors competent to work therapeutically with a range of clients, short and long term, to a high standard of ethical, professional and personal integrity. It is right to say that, as yet, not all courses reach this standard. In terms of personal development, all the issues and elements identified so far in short courses and certificate level courses are likely to be present, with the addition of further core features and vehicles for personal work. From selection onwards, the person of the trainee, her qualities, strengths and areas of weakness must be in focus. If counselling is primarily a therapeutic alliance (Garfield and Bergin, 1986) as outlined in Chapter 1, then the person of the counsellor and the nature of the relationships she is able to forge are crucial. What then is it reasonable to ask for in potential counsellors? For our own postgraduate diplomas, as one element of the selection criteria, we expect the personal qualities which have been identified as central in counselling:

- warmth of personality
- flexibility of thinking
- the capacity for sensitive response to a wide range of people and issues
- the ability to argue critically and evaluate ideas and outcomes.

Other courses with different orientations might add to or subtract from those specific elements, highlighting aspects of their approach in particular ways; for our courses, built on person–centred values and working within an integrated skills model applied to both short and long term work with clients, students must be able to feel, think, relate, communicate, evaluate ... and grow, since we also demand 'a commitment to self evaluation and self development' – both personally and professionally. And this is one of the significant differences in personal development work at this level of training; the interrelationship of personal and professional, the application of self-development in a vocational context, the constant reminder that work on self is in the service of work with clients, whatever indirect benefits or costs accrue to the individual counsellor/human being. The BAC Course Recognition Guidelines suggest that candidates for counselling training be considered in the light of the following criteria:

1. Self awareness and stability.
2. Ability to make use of and reflect upon life experience.
3. Capacity to cope with the emotional demands of the course.
4. Ability to cope with intellectual and academic requirements.
5. Ability to form a helping relationship.

6. Ability to be self critical and use both positive and negative feedback.
7. Have an awareness of the nature of prejudice and oppression of minority groups.

In any kind of counselling training, personal growth is possible, desirable and likely (or I would be very suspicious of the quality and focus of such work); where training is intended to produce qualified, competent counsellors, then personal development – purposeful, focused, aimed at building strengths, modifying or at least clarifying limitations and extending range, all in the service of the clients – must be a central driving energy in the course structure.

MODES WITHIN A COURSE

The personal development work to meet these needs and build on those criteria can operate in four modes within a course:

- Discrete and specific within the course, labelled as personal development through focused activities, undertaken at some depth in groups, structured exercises and in individual tasks.
- Through reflection on, implications for and application to the individual of all other elements of the course, such as skills work, feedback opportunities, theoretical and conceptual study, and assessment experience.
- Through the learning from and application of supervision of direct work with clients.
- Through the individual student's experience as a client in personal counselling/therapy.

These will all be discussed further in Chapters 7, 8 and 9. It is noticeable that whereas there is considerable debate about the place of personal counselling for trainees, there is little argument about the centrality of supervision in a diploma level course, as the BAC Codes stress. For the purposes of personal development, the significance of supervision, combined with tutor and peer feedback, can be to highlight blind spots or vulnerabilities, to identify sensitive trigger points in past or present experience and to explore, in a safe and supportive climate, intra- and interpersonal issues stimulated or restimulated by clients. Ultimately, the skills and insights developed here should also be internalized into a parallel capacity for self monitoring, the 'internal supervisor' described so eloquently by Casement (1985) and developed and reinforced by such training approaches as Interpersonal Process Recall (Kagan, 1967, see Chapter 8). Part of this work involves the identifying of issues more appropriate for personal counselling. Although engagement as a client in personal counselling/therapy is generally regarded as important in training at this Diploma/Masters level – a significant difference from shorter less rigorous courses – there are a number of aspects that can be debated. There is little research evidence (Aveline, 1990) to prove the effectiveness of personal counselling for counsellors in training, yet the anecdotal value of the experience for both personal and professional development is unchallenged and most trainers would say it is essential. The questions which arise include when this experience is most useful: 'readiness' for training is a key element of selection, and experience as a client before embarking on a course is often seen a prerequisite for selection. Such experience should have helpfully stimulated awareness, curiosity and some self-knowledge and perhaps begun the process of self-acceptance. However, if the process occurs too near the start of the counsellor training course, then the trainee may feel too exposed, vulnerable or disturbed in some way, particularly if her or his client material has centred around a life crisis such as bereavement or loss of any kind. A similar dichotomy of views can be identified concerning the place of personal counselling during a course: some trainers (especially in some theoretical approaches) see it as vital for the duration of the training, as the appropriate forum for dealing in depth with any material triggered by the course, while others argue that that can lead to an avoidance of issues being dealt with where they belong – in the course itself, with course members, in a climate of appropriate support and challenge, facilitated by responsible tutors. The timing of much personal counselling may well come into the frame again at the end of a substantial training course, in preparation for the individual's 'after life' as a professional counsellor. The course may be seen as having a duty to encourage counsellors to maintain an existing or seek a new personal counselling relationship as a crucial safety net of support for the strains and stresses of survival as a counsellor. It is likely, too, to play a significant part, with supervision, in further professional and personal development. In terms of timing, what may matter most is making the choice, voluntarily undertaking the experience, rather than simply fulfilling someone else's requirement – a process in keeping with the values of counselling. (For further discussion, see Chapter 7.)

A further issue for debate centres around questions of congruence and similarity or difference: in order to optimize personal development, should the model of personal counselling be identical with, similar to or different than the core theoretical and practical orientation of a course itself? The advantages of congruence and of similarity centre around coherence, reinforcement of learning and clarity, while differences in models provide helpfully different perspectives and allow for evaluation, comparison and questioning. Questions of the value of congruence and similarity or of contrast can also be applied to the gender of the counsellor and client, ethnicity, age, class and sexual orientation. It is doubtful whether there can be absolute answers: it seems likely that too much difference, on any variable, may produce confusion, especially for counsellors relatively early in their training;

on the other hand, comparisons, some dissonance and a range of viewpoints can, with sufficient opportunities for clarifying the learning, be valuable stepping stones to understanding. My own experiences of being a client, no matter when, where, how or what, have been some of the most fruitful learning opportunities for me as a person and as a counsellor; and different experiences as a client over my own professional life have reinforced that view, as I have been ready to risk new bites at the process: readiness is all!

There is little argument about the importance of personal development in Diploma/Masters level training, integrated and discrete, through all these avenues of course activities, supervision and personal counselling. The need for and valuing of such work has strengthened the rationale for course groups of a reasonable size – despite pressures for income generation – and for those groups to be coherent and stable over the duration of the course. Movements towards modularization, APL and APEL (accreditation of prior learning and prior experiential learning) may threaten this pattern of provision and could dramatically dilute the effectiveness of personal development work in higher education and commercial contexts.

Personal development, in terms of courses with different aims or set at different levels, can be seen as central, inevitably developmental and triggered in many ways. As a trainee emphasized recently at the end of her two year Diploma course:

> *If I'd known when I began the training, that I would need to explore and face so many unexpected aspects of myself, I might never have started! In the first year it felt like being in one of those giant mazes – if only I had had a ball of string to guide me out! Then, this year, some of the blocked paths seemed to open out; I've been able to move faster and feel more sure-footed, and I mind less not being able to 'know it all' about myself. In fact, my life now feels more like a detective story – and I love 'the thrill of the chase!'*

SOME QUESTIONS

1. Reflect on any counselling training you know well: evaluate the balance of work on self, in relation to theory and skills.

2. What elements in counselling training help and which block personal development?

3. Is it possible to define minimum levels of personal development, whatever the level and purpose of a counselling course?

4. In relation to personal development, what kinds of issues are raised around assessment?

THREE

Through the looking glass?

Theoretical differences and personal development

One of the most significant ways in which courses differ is in their theoretical, philosophical and values base. Much energy, debate, critical thought and even, at times, hostile exchange have been expended on these differences of approach. While diversity in most human activities is encouraged, single theory approaches to counselling have been for a long time in vogue and indeed often, it seems, each presented as the (unproven) 'holy grail' in terms of counselling outcomes. Yet, as McLeod (1993) points out: 'There is some evidence that practitioners who claim to use different approaches to counselling may work with clients in an identical manner and that there can be huge differences between practitioners who purport to employ the same model.'

There are now many approaches to and schools of counselling, including major moves in the last twenty years towards eclectic and especially integrative models. There is some degree of consensus that the relationship between client and counsellor and therefore the person of the counsellor are key in all models, as evidenced by the BAC (1990) and BPS (1995) course recognition guides and requirements. The three principal approaches of psychodynamic, person-centred and cognitive-behavioural counselling contain, however, some significantly different 'images of the person' and ways of being effectively and maladaptively human (see McLeod, 1993; Nelson-Jones, 1982; Patterson, 1986; Nye, 1986). These are bound to influence personal development work in each approach. McLeod helpfully suggests metaphors which reflect something of the beliefs about the essence of a client in each:

- psychodynamic – animal, driven by instinct and out of control;
- humanistic – botanical, growing in helpful or unhelpful conditions;
- cognitive-behavioural – computer like, mechanistic, badly programmed.

Other social, economic, class, gender and religious assumptions are also embedded in the different approaches. Inevitably then, in the training courses for counselling of different schools, personal development will occupy a range of positions. It is impossible here to tease out all the implications for the different ways of managing such work; it is likely that trainers probably themselves trained in the same orientation will perpetuate a similar model. I shall try, in the next section to suggest a few key questions and their relevance for personal development. The dangers of over simplification and distortion are obvious!

Psychodynamic approaches to counselling

Jacobs (1988) defines 'psychodynamic' as the ways in which 'the psyche (as minds/emotion/spirit/self) is seen as active and not static' both within the person and between people. Traditionally the closer these therapeutic ways of working have been to their psychoanalytic origins, then the counselling has tended towards longer term, years rather than months, based on frequent sessions, focusing on the client's unconscious processes, the effects and meaning of past personal history, exploring defences and neuroses. The core therapeutic processes are the use of the transference relationship, interpretation and working with defences and resistance, based around elaborate theories of child development and life stages, which are very detailed and can seem prescriptive. There have been many modifications over time: for example, in the acceptance of methods of brief psychodynamic therapy; the recognition of the real relationship as also significant in creating a working alliance; and the weight given to emotion as well as intellect and reason. Essentially, though, the real work in psychodynamic counselling is done through transference, an 'as if' relationship which allows the client through his relationship with the counsellor to relive, explore and rework significant relationships from her past. Transference can be positive or negative, both in the nature of the past feelings and the effect on the counselling relationship. The counsellor's particular skill lies in the timing, use and degree of interpretation about the client's transference reactions and the use of any connections in the 'triangle of insight' – past/then/parent/child – present/here and now/counsellor–client – present/out there/client–others. A further key strand of psychodynamic counselling lies in the counsellor's understanding and use in the counselling relationship of her own counter–transference feelings and reactions: anything evoked by the client but rooted in the counsellor's own past and own difficulties or patterns. These may be hard to separate from the real feelings stimulated by the client in the moment. (See Jacobs (1988) for a succinct exploration of transference and counter–transference.) Clear boundaries, in order to provide firm authority, holding and containment, are also significant in this approach.

Training for working with a psychodynamic model has always had at its centre mandatory experience of individual therapy, as itself part of the training process. Heavy stress is often laid on this, with particular emphasis on the match between the individual's experience of therapy and the core training model. This then is the main vehicle for personal development work, with exploration of patterns, the past, childhood experiences and issues, blind spots and potential fertile ground for counter transference.

Despite the fact that the counsellor in this model deliberately keeps him or herself as a fellow human being in the background – or because of it – the counsellor must keep asking: 'What does it – (this mood, that action, this memory, that feeling, this aspect of our relationship, that symbol, this defence, that explanation) – what does it mean?' (Jacobs, 1988) ... and must ask it of the client and of himself. Many post- Freudian models of psychodynamic therapy and counselling acknowledge that 'the ideal of impersonal behaviour on the part of the therapist must be modified. The therapist (read counsellor) should not aim to be a blank screen but should behave in the way patients (read clients)would expect of one to whom they have come for help' (Patterson, 1986). This is particularly so in the brief therapy approaches and in others where a 'corrective emotional experience' for the client (Alexander and French, in McLeod, 1993) may be a key element in the process – to allow feelings in the presence of the counsellor which have previously been unacceptable. In parallel, the counsellor may also experience a range of here-and-now feelings for which he or she will need strategies. Similarly, the use of transference is different in brief therapy approaches, with here-and-now feelings and relationship again being more significant. The ability to create and maintain a 'working alliance' is at least as valuable as managing a transference relationship. All of this should increase the significance of self-awareness work in psychodynamic training and also the need for opportunities for would-be psychodynamic counsellors to experience direct relationships and feedback about their 'real' interpersonal effectiveness. They might achieve these through the range of personal development activities found in other models as well as those traditional in psychodynamic training. Crucially, counsellors training in a psychodynamic model must be able to distinguish between emotions, attitudes, intra- or interpersonal conflicts that stem from their own 'unfinished business' and life history and reactions and responses triggered by the transference relationship with the client. They must beware, too, of the potentially abusive power of the 'expert' role.

A further challenge might be to ask psychodynamic counsellors to loosen their use of the detailed structure of psychodynamic theories for understanding human life and development; to use such frameworks as guides, sources for questions, rather than templates to 'measure' people; to diverge from such theories creatively and imaginatively and be open to the uniqueness of individuals rather than to generalise about clients slotted into theories. Personal development in such training might then need to cope with far more uncertainty, anxiety and 'not knowing' in trainees, who had expected to be authority figures, taking refuge in an aloof, cold, distant style, reliant on authoritarian interpretation. It is, of course, likely that the more insecure or inexperienced trainees are, the more rigidly they will want to cling to the ideological purity of their model – and that will be true of trainees in any approach to counselling! As with all theoretical orientations, the fascinating question seems to be: 'Who is attracted to this model and why?'!

Person-centred approaches to counselling

Some distorted presentations of person-centred counselling claim that counsellors give away their power as 'experts' and aim 'merely' to be equal human beings with their clients, thus denying at once malign influence and potential for good. Any training which reinforces these views should be challenged for perpetuating false myths. The reality is that person-centred counselling, developed through the work of Carl Rogers and others, is a highly concentrated and committed process in which one individual puts all her resources, including herself within ethical limits, at the service of another who is seeking help. Key tenets include the quality of the counselling relationship itself, a valuing of the subjective reality of every individual's experience, assumptions that all human beings can take responsibility for their own lives, are capable of positive change and growth and have inner resources which they can use for self-awareness, self-understanding and self-acceptance. The person-centred counsellor has expertise, but must, as Mearns and Thorne (1988) say, 'learn to wear her expertise as an invisible garment', since trusting the client's own ability to learn, choose, move is central to the approach. 'Experts' – from parents onwards – in the client's life have been instrumental and often destructive in creating a limiting and distorted self-concept through loving only conditionally. We are all in different degrees, victims of 'conditions of worth' and spend our lives seeking approval and fearing rejection; this struggle cuts us off from our 'real', or 'organismic' self, which person-centred counsellors believe can and will grow in healthy ways, given appropriate nurturing conditions and support. Becoming a 'fully functioning person' (Rogers, 1963) involves a process of learning to trust our inner selves and be able to live vividly in the present, evaluating the 'oughts and shoulds', often coming from other people's voices inside us, which can so easily dominate our lives. Confusion and unhappiness, in contrast, are created and maintained when we can only sustain our picture of ourselves by denying inner messages and being deaf to core needs, depending meanwhile on the 'positive judgement of others for a sense of self-worth.' (See Mearns and Thorne (1988) for a fuller discussion; Rogers, 1961; Patterson, 1986.)

It is the counsellor's task to offer more effective 'conditions of growth' through a reparative loving relationship, which Rogers and others believe is characterized by the counsellor's ability to communicate consistently the so-called three 'core conditions': congruence or genuineness, being real transparent and human in the relationship; unconditional positive regard or acceptance, a non-judgemental respect for the client; and empathic understanding, the capacity to move around in the client's world, to feel and perceive for the moment as the client does, to share the client's personal meanings.

What then are the training implications, particularly for personal development, in person-centred counselling? As Mearns and Thorne (1988) stress, 'The investment of the self of the counsellor in the therapy process cannot be over-emphasised'. Unlike most models of helping which commend objectivity and detachment, person-centred counsellors believe that it is their 'ability to become involved and to share (their) client's world which will determine (their) effectiveness' (Mearns and Thorne, 1988). In parallel with the 'relatively light theoretical framework' (McLeod, 1994) and the absence to some degree of a skills/techniques focus, training for a person-centred approach must concentrate on the attitudes, philosophy, qualities, beliefs and 'ways of being' of the counsellor herself. Personal development work then is central and focuses on the counsellor working:

- to identify her own needs, fears and blocks to self-acceptance and self love – and therefore her acceptance of others;
- to uncover and challenge the counsellor's implicit personal theories about human growth and development, so that theories and beliefs can be used helpfully, not as predictions for individuals to fit into;
- towards being centred, stability, congruence in the counsellor of all aspects of her own experience;
- to use opportunities to release sensitivity so that empathic responsiveness to others is increased.

Learning to listen to and hear their own confusions, to struggle for self-acceptance and appreciate vulnerability and inadequacy, guilt and shame, are central, if counsellors are truly to share the humanity of their clients and yet be clear about their differences from them, as well as their similarities. Personal development work for counsellors, then, will involve extending their range of familiarity with the breadth of human experience, through risking new experiences, reading widely, and stimulating their imagination – all with a view to extending acceptance of others and the capacity for empathic response. Most of all, person-centred counsellors in training will need to work towards being consistently genuine and open, not only in the therapeutic encounter, with all the risks of consequent turbulence, change, transition and difficulty in their own relationships and personal world. The experience of being in the training group and in one-to-one work with peers will reinforce all this. (For further discussion see Chapters 7, 8 and 9.) Being open about purpose and intention, demystifying the counselling process, explaining to clients the principles, values and commitments of person-centred counselling are all intrinsic to the way of working and need to be practised in training; similarly the skills of empathic communication, self-disclosure and immediacy have to be worked on and used in training, integrated with personal development process and focus. Most counsellors from many orientations now accept that the core conditions are necessary to build a high quality working alliance, even if some also believe they are not sufficient. In the person-centred model, with that central belief, the task of training for such an intensified use of self must also include preparation for burn-out, the ability to recognize one's own limits, the feeding needed to survive being and staying close to people in pain, distress and anger, the strength to tolerate real hostility, love or rejection in the moment ... unprotected by professional role and distance, although within ethical limits.

What are the criticisms and dangers here that need to be addressed in training? Antagonists to the person-centred approach sometimes attack the 'niceness' of counsellors; are suspicious of their warmth and openness as 'too good to be true'; are hostile to the apparent simplicity and lack of structure. Some clients feel frustrated by the lack of direction offered by the counsellor or, conversely, feel seduced into a 'folie a deux', a joint madness of positive thinking. Personal development work must offer trainees in person-centred training the opportunity to confront these challenges and to question their own hidden agendas around implicit power and control, disguised, at worst, by attractive concepts denying the very existence of such monsters. As Strong's (1968) social influence theory reminds us, the more a client perceives a counsellor to be attractive, trustworthy and expert – even at being not the expert! – the more power and influence the counsellor is likely to possess. This paradox is at the heart of personal development work in person-centred counselling training.

Cognitive-Behavioural Counselling

McLeod (1994) outlines the key features of cognitive-behavioural counselling as: 'a problem-solving, change-focused approach to working with clients; a respect for scientific values and close attention to the cognitive processes through which people monitor and control their behaviour'. Although practitioners in this model, as in all approaches, now pay more attention to the client–counsellor relationship, its purpose is less for exploration, understanding and insight than towards client action to produce change or solve problems. The approach is much more technique orientated, with interventions, strategies, programmes managed and controlled by the counsellor, sometimes called the 'scientist-practitioner'. The model stresses the value of ways of thinking and of learning principles; the counsellor is seen as an educator/teacher offering skills for the client to learn; and it concentrates on the present and future rather than the past and the client's experiences outside the counselling room rather than the relationship within it. Some critics attack the approach as being more of 'a technology than a framework for understanding life' (McLeod, 1993), yet concepts such as self-defeating thinking; that unrealistic and negative beliefs (not facts) lead to emotional distress or disorder; and that irrational beliefs can dominate lives and stop people achieving their goals have been very helpful in many counselling frameworks. Cognitive-behavioural counselling is aimed at helping clients to identify and modify maladaptive thinking; undertake tasks which help them test out their false thinking and learn more realistic thinking; and work for change to allow a consequent significant shift in feeling and behaviour (see Trower *et al.*, 1988) for a clear outline of the core principles and practice of cognitive-behavioural counselling).

Significant features of this approach are that it is a collaborative skills-training model, with the counsellor's primary task to 'teach clients the skills necessary for them to identify and modify their own self-defeating thoughts and beliefs' (Trower *et al.*, 1988). Sometimes attacked for not dealing sufficiently with emotion and states of distress, the model does accept that people's lives are damaged by dysfunctional emotions, but is committed to the view that these are caused by self-defeating negative or irrational thoughts. Strengths of the approach include:

- a focus on the present experience of the client;
- reality checking and challenges to catastrophic thinking;
- creativity and skills in designing activities, tasks and challenges which engage the client in collaborative self-help – itself sometimes raising energy and modifying a negative view of self;
- and working constructively with blocks to change and towards independence.

Critics of the cognitive-behavioural approach have focused on the lack of attention paid to the past and to childhood experiences, to unconscious processes and to the actual relationship between the client and counsellor. The cognitive-behavioural approach to the significance of past events lies in the philosopher Epictetus' view that 'Men are disturbed not by things but by the views which they take of them'. Again, it is argued that the therapeutic relationship is significant, counselling skills and empathy are important, but as the backdrop to managing therapeutic tasks, rather than as ends in themselves or as a primary vehicle for change. Dryden (1991) describes the task of a rational-emotive counsellor, similar in essence to a cognitive-behavioural counsellor, as 'to establish and maintain an appropriate bonded relationship that will encourage each individual client to implement his or her goal-directed tasks'. His view is that different clients need different kinds of 'bonded' relationships; hence his focus is on observation of clients' needs, cues and responses rather than on himself. Similarly he argues for a range of styles, matching degrees of client passivity, within the necessarily active and directive conduct of cognitive-behavioural counselling. Dryden stresses that 'Unlike the majority of counsellors of my acquaintance, I do not regard the relationship between counsellor and client to be the sine qua non of effective counselling.' This attitude seems consistent with the general view of cognitive behavioural counsellors that, 'The good cognitive-behavioural counsellor will be skilfully monitoring the therapeutic relationship throughout the course of the counselling', attempting 'to assess interpersonal beliefs while resisting being drawn into reacting to the client's behaviour' (Trower *et al.*, 1988).

What does all this mean in the training of cognitive-behavioural counsellors and, in particular, in any personal development work? Compared with the stress in psychodynamic approaches on transference, insight and the unconscious and in person-centred counselling on the self of the counsellor and the warmth of a real interpersonal relationship, the different emphasis here suggests a very different balance. The emphasis in training is on a primary understanding of *thinking* processes, of how people learn and change patterns of thinking and hence feelings and behaviour, and on skills, techniques, strategies, action-orientated processes. There seems relatively little attention paid to the impact on the client of the person of the counsellor. There is rather an assumption that an equal-adult, collaborative working relationship can be set up almost automatically, regardless of the counsellor's effect on the perceptions, needs, feelings and interpersonal relationship issues which the client brings to counselling and which virtually every other model of counselling sees as significant and central. There is, usually, no expectation that cognitive-behavioural counsellors will undergo personal counselling/therapy as part of their training; where there is evidence of attention to awareness, it is focused outwards rather than inwards, on observation of cues from the client rather than on any internal processes, feelings, or responses of the counsellor. McLeod (1993) points out that there is no theoretical concept in cognitive-behavioural counselling equivalent to counter-transference or to congruence, despite professed attention to the importance of a successful working alliance.

McLeod also raises the question of the weight, effects and appropriateness of challenge and confrontation, embedded as they are at the heart of the cognitive-behavioural counselling approach. If counsellors in training pay insufficient attention to exploration and awareness of their own needs and motives, then such challenge can be for the wrong reasons, in response to some inner drive of the counsellor rather than to needs in the client. Questions then arise around manipulation, oppression and potential abuse of power, personality or motivation. There is a further concern, given the explicit emphasis in this approach on persuasion, influence and direction of the client: ethical issues around control, self-responsibility and integrity should be explored; attention is given in cognitive-behavioural counselling writings to helping the client towards autonomy, yet the 'expert' stance of the counsellor and its potential for prescriptive influence seems implicitly unchallenged. It is interesting to note that Trower *et al.* (1988) stress three counsellor qualities to help create 'rapport': empathic understanding, unconditional positive regard ... so far, so similar ... and then replace genuineness with confidence! Training, then, aims to build self-esteem and a sense of being expert: very different from the humility (however hard to achieve!) advocated by person-centred therapists. Where attention is given in training to boundaries, the aim is to 'ensure a framework of objectivity ... and ensure the counsellor stays on the periphery of the client's actual life' (Trower *et al.*, 1988). This is clearly important, but it is a very different focus in its attention to time and duration of sessions than to emotional facets of the counsellor, unfinished business which might be tapped or counter-transference issues. The aim is to avoid being drawn into 'the kind of dysfunctional relationship which may have contributed to the clients problem in the first place' – again very different from either the exploration of the transference relationship or the real counsellor/client relationship in the other models. The emphasis is on control, management and appropriate distance. Techniques and skills are used to hold the frame, involving challenge, disputatious argument and rational exchange – at every stage of the counselling process, even the very ending itself.

The potential dangers seem quite great of cognitive-behavioural counsellors being, at the worst, arrogant and unaware of what needs of their own are being met. They may, too, have had insufficient experience of emotion and affect as clients themselves to empathize adequately with others or to develop ethically sound, therapeutically effective counsellor–client relationships. At the same time, their training and personal development work may have strengthened their creativity, imaginative application of techniques and deepened their understanding of maladaptive thought processes in themselves and others. Cognitive-behavioural counsellors should be able to focus, be concrete, and enable clients to move beyond insight and felt experience to tangible behaviour change and productive problem solving, yet their own personal development and hence that of their clients may be limited and narrow.

These and other counselling models

In terms of theoretical orientation, and personal development, several questions seem most pertinent: firstly, for each training orientation:

- What kind of person is attracted to it and why?
- What is the successful match of personal strengths with the particular emphasis of different orientations?
- What is the shadow side?
- Which combination of trainee characteristics and training emphasis might produce dangerous, damaging or disturbing counsellors?

Secondly, if you are a counsellor or trainer who espouses a particular model or approach, ask yourself:

- How, in your training, your own personal development was prompted (or not!); what were the missed opportunities?
- What was specific and connected with the core model and what was incidental?
- How and where were you encouraged to make all the connections?

Thirdly, it may be useful to ask all these questions of other models of counselling to identify the significant and discrete personal development elements in their different trainings. For example, from psychosynthesis, concepts such as selfhood, the transpersonal, higher consciousness, the challenges and obstacles in the way of each individual fulfilling her purpose in life, peak experiences and the therapeutic styles of 'love' and 'will': how might these translate in training into work on personal development? In training for existential counselling, what appropriate and specific work on self might prepare the trainee counsellor for the essential existential task of clarifying, reflecting upon and understanding life, for finding and valuing an individual's meaning and purpose in existence, for enabling someone to think through the unthinkable, and for avoiding the presumption of being a mature sage full of wisdom? In gestalt training, how can trainees be helped to focus on and improve their imperfect awareness and work towards an integration of the different parts of themselves?

And so on for any model or approach to counselling: the task is to identify the key elements of philosophy and practice, then weave a training web of appropriate work on personal development which incorporates all the common elements described earlier, while capturing the specific differences, colourings and beliefs that each approach to counselling encapsulates. For courses which claim to be eclectic or integrative, such a task, in terms of course design, is even more central: to identify potential contradictions in theory and practice; to find means of articulating the connections between the aims of counselling and the counsellor's strengths and potential; and to work with the paradoxes inherent in synthesising differences in setting, levels and theories is truly challenging.

THE TRAINING COURSE AS AN ENTITY

No two counselling courses are alike: and I have looked at them from many perspectives – as a student/trainee in the dim and distant past, as a trainer/counsellor now for many years, as an HMI in the early 1980s with national responsibility for counselling, as an external examiner and as a member of BAC course recognition panels. The same theme, expressed earlier in this chapter, persists: common elements will underpin all, yet differences, overall and in the commitment to personal development, will distinguish one from another. Those overall differences will be to do with the teaching and learning philosophy of the course, the understanding of and willingness to meet adult learning needs, some balance of the person, skills, values, style, competence and charisma of the trainer/s, the composition and elements of the course design and the particular configuration, 'gestalt', of all the facets of the course. These are expressed both through explicit course description (how easy or difficult it is to get the 'feel' of a course from reading a course brochure?!) and through the implicit messages from structure, prioritizing, time, commitment, staff attitudes and differences which become visible between stated and actual course provision. Inconsistencies will fatally undermine the credibility of a course: person-centred courses whose staff are authoritarian and oppressive towards trainees or psychodynamic courses where boundaries are messy and inconsistent are self-sabotaging and unethical in what they offer trainees.

I shall return in later chapters to issues of learning and teaching models and how they might specifically contribute to the personal development of trainee counsellors. Here, it seems important to recognize that all personal development is about the ways in which we learn and change, and that any change, in knowledge, skills, attitude or awareness, usually influences the whole person. Any learning, almost inevitably, involves both excitement and anxiety, with their accompanying need for both support and challenge – support to manage the anxiety and challenge to focus the excitement (Clark, 1991). The most effective trainer will be able to offer an appropriate helping relationship (Rogers, 1983) of trust, worth, patience and respect and also be a 'change-agent' stimulating growth and movement in particular purposeful directions. Trainers in counselling (see Chapter 6) are very varied in background, skills, experience, style and values; the courses they lead will reflect some of those differences and illustrate in action the complex interplay of course content and focus, trainer ability and style and trainee response and potential for learning.

However all those variables operate, all courses will in themselves affect the personal development of course members through the following elements:

- trainer modelling (for good or ill)
- teaching and learning models and processes
- self/peer/tutor feedback opportunities
- assessment and evaluation methods
- group and community process
- explicit and implicit values communicated by the course and its setting
- content of theory and practice
- the myriad ways in which course members survive the roller-coaster of increasing and decreasing self-esteem as they negotiate their own learning journey through the life-history of the course.

This chapter has attempted to identify some of the key differences in theoretical orientations and learning climates. It is essential to recognize, too, that much personal development for any of us, trainers, trainees, counsellors, clients, comes not from training but from life, human experience, personal relationships and other learning arenas such as literature, art and music. As Emmy van Deurzen–Smith (1992) says, ' ... I am, beyond training and self-understanding, bound by the same existential dilemmas as my clients. It is a fact of life that we are never perfectly equipped to help others and we are never exempt from the human condition in which we intervene.'

SOME QUESTIONS

1. What aspects of theory influence your understanding of personal development?

2. In your theoretical orientation as a counsellor, what elements of personal development seem essential to enable you to work effectively?

3. Should counsellors-in-training fail or be asked to leave a course for reasons only to do with personal development? How does that match with person-centred values around growth, change and potential for 'becoming'?

4. What boundaries is it always unacceptable for counsellors to break?

FOUR

Who are the characters?

Trainees and their personal development: a crowded stage?

Underpinning any exploration of personal development is Satir's (1972) assertion that 'There is always hope that your life can change because you can always learn new things.' That theme recurs throughout this book, counterpointing her other key motif, that 'integrity, honesty, responsibility, compassion, love', all come more easily from people who have high self-esteem, constructed from the valuing of others, combined with self-knowledge and, crucially, self-acceptance. As Connor (1994) asserts, 'a positive and realistic concept of the self-as-counsellor is at the core' of any training model. This chapter and the next two will suggest some frameworks for considering personal development. This chapter will explore what *trainees* bring and need, what content and issues are triggered in a substantial training course; Chapter 5 will outline possible objectives and some of the main themes of personal development; and in Chapter 6, the roles and personal development needs of *trainers* and the nature and contribution of the learning group will be explored.

At times, any counselling course seems like a complex drama or opera, with a large cast, an improvised plot, shifts of power and influence amongst characters, backstage politics, tantrums and so on. In any drama, much of the interest centres on the protagonists, their natures, relationships, needs and development. So, for counselling training: whatever the 'story' embodied in the design, form and plan of the course, the actual lived experience of the process will be transmuted through and coloured by the group of individuals (an inevitable paradox!) who make up the course community. Those individuals will directly dictate, within whatever partly predetermined framework, the nature, depth and focus of personal development work undertaken. Much will depend on their separate and collective 'ages and stages', developmental and crisis experiences, personal histories, current life space, attitudes, perceptions and degrees of maturity; and on their 'significant others'. In the course meeting room will be at various times all the people whose shadows and echoes accompany course members (and trainers) in the group, birth-families and present families of whatever kind, conventional or alternative, clients, enemies, authority figures, colleagues, friends, past or present lovers, anyone with whom any individual has current or unfinished business – a crowded stage indeed!

In order to have some sense of who is involved and what their needs are in this task of personal growth for counsellors-in-training, this chapter will offer some frameworks for capturing aspects of trainees' existence and development. The key question is, as Jersild (1955) encapsulated it, 'Who am I and who can I be for others?'

Trainees

It is impossible in the space available to analyse all possible aspects of being a trainee; that would involve all the implications of being human, psychological, sociological, existential, spiritual, physical, sexual, vocational and transpersonal. It is, of course, a reality of the immense task and responsibility embedded in counselling training that all those elements are present and should not be evaded. The focus here, however, is on some concepts and structures that seem particularly helpful in grasping the implications of and for personal development work. Of particular significance are ages and stages, life space, transitions, the interaction of personal awareness with individual needs, group needs and tasks, and the effects of working with clients.

Ages and stages

Trainees/students in counselling are invariably beyond their first youth! Most courses have, if not a minimum age limit (generally around 25), then at least some expectation of maturity in experience if not in chronological years. I have been challenged – uncomfortably – by prospective candidates for our Diploma course, who are in their early twenties, and who have rightly argued for the complexity and understanding of their brief life experience, in comparison with a shallow forty year old who has repeated one year of adult life twenty times! Some degree of maturity, however, and the capacity to reflect on it are significant in providing a solid base from which to manage the turbulence of being again in a learning role and the pressures which clients and counselling can bring. The majority of course members, certainly on lengthy courses, are in their thirties and forties, with some older (the oldest member of a Diploma course in my experience has been a nun of over seventy) and a very small number in their late twenties.

Much of the framework for 'age and stage' considerations stems from the work of psychologists such as Super, in vocational development, Havighurst, Levinson, Maslow and Allport, together with the child development theories of Freud and Piaget (all in Sugarman, 1986). All have some use in stimulating questions, comparisons or contrasts, but must always be challenged for cultural, gender or ethnic bias. The best known framework for psychosocial development is Erikson's (1980), whose concept of 'identity and the life cycle' has underpinned much later thinking (see Sugarman, 1986; Woolf and Sugarman, 1989). Erikson outlined eight life stages, with crises and tasks associated with each; and argued that failure to complete successfully these tasks may lead to later difficulties. (This links too with psychodynamic descriptions of unresolved conflicts or gestalt's notions of unfinished business.) Trainees in their thirties, forties and fifties are struggling with all the issues of making life meaningful, living out their values, coping creatively with work, families and self-fulfilment, perhaps feeling blocked, uncertain or purposeless, or in personal and work relationships that have not lived up to earlier ideals or hopes. At the same time they are on a course which is demanding academically and emotionally and which may well bring up earlier issues of competence as a learner, such as fear and low self-esteem or relationship-building issues such as capacity for closeness and needs for distance.

Consider, for instance, these two trainees, members of the same course group, describing some 'facts' about themselves in an exercise half-way through their training:

Andrew: I'm 32; married for three years, with a child aged one. My partner, Jean, works full-time in a high-powered job in finance. She earns more than I do, since I've opted out of promotion in order to do the course – and, anyway, I'm a psychiatric nurse! We live close to my parents, who are about to retire. My main interest other than work has always been rugby, but I've just given up playing and feel I'm losing my friends as well. I just haven't a clue what I might be doing in five years time, but I worry that our marriage won't cope with all the pressures we seem to be under at present.

That is a vivid picture of a young man with a great deal to grapple with; contrast his life-stage, with all its issues, with the following:

Sarah: I was widowed suddenly seven years ago, when I was 48; I was already working as a counsellor with a voluntary agency. My two children both live in Scotland. The hardest decision for me at the moment is whether to move up there when I finish the course. My mother is also widowed and has heart trouble. I've coped with so many new experiences in the last few years and feel quite tired of facing everything on my own.

This is rich and valuable material, but sometimes it is hard for trainees to handle; the frameworks and commitment to time for and focus on personal development may be vital.

Life-span developmental psychology, as a way of framing human life, can be attacked for being too prescriptive and normative; if used sensitively and openly, for many counselling trainees the insights and comparisons which emerge are often very fruitful and allow people the opportunity to re-evaluate their present, review the past and explore future development within a stimulating conceptual framework. Sharing specific experiences, similarities and differences linked with ages and stages, and exploring, for example, cross-cultural or gender contrasts are productive processes, which challenge many assumptions and help expose underlying attitudes and expectations. In terms of the contribution to personal development work, the key assumptions of the life-span approach are the expectation of life-long change, the identification of generic skills and the possibility of building resources for dealing with the unexpected.

Some of the most productive personal development work can come from the sense of comparison which courses can prompt, not only with other people, but with our unconscious pictures and expectations of ourselves, as well as from increased awareness and openness to other people's perceptions of us. As Woolf and Sugarman (1989) point out, age and ageing, for example, are constants in our lives, affecting us physically, cognitively and emotionally, yet we are often unaware of the process until some sudden insight into our sameness with or differences from someone else – or with our own internal picture – shocks us into a new self perception and sense of identity. Seeing old photos of myself with dark brown hair can jolt me in this way, as can the realisation that, however much affinity I feel with a new thirty year old colleague, that I could be her mother – and she may be seeing me as such! Similarly, some trainees can feel out of step with the expected timing of events or life patterns, for example, in our culture not having married or bought a house or not having children or a permanent job at, say, thirty-five. As always, it is less the events themselves, rather our perception or reframing of them which causes emotional reactions and allows issues for personal development work to emerge. At the same time, challenging assumptions about age or stage changes and expectations allows us to notice how the world around us is changing too and how, in particular, clients may be different in a myriad of ways than we expect them to be.

Life space

Trainees are social beings, not only in their interactions within the course, but also in all the baggage they bring with them in terms of family history, educational experiences, present personal, social and work existences – and their thoughts, feelings, anxieties, fears and desires about them all.

Most mature adults creating space for intensive training are under great pressure of conflicting time demands, responsibilities, work expectations, family, social or other commitments. However much they want to undertake the course, clashes around priorities and conflicts of oughts and shoulds will unavoidably create stresses and strains. Tensions are possible too between the needs of other people, the 'significant others', in the trainees' personal world and the absorption (if not, at times, obsession) of the trainee within the esoteric climate of the course. Students sometimes comment on how differently they relate and communicate on the course compared with how they are at home or at work, where they may well be locked into old patterns and others' fixed expectations of them. The strains and conflicts which can arise in complex, busy lives are illustrated by a simple exercise, recently undertaken with a new certificate group. One trainee, for instance, felt she lived out an astonishing number of roles:

> *I think I am, at different times, all the following – and lots of them at the same time! I am mother, daughter of ageing father, partner, lover, dog-owner, friend, ballroom dancer, teacher, local councillor, poetry writer, school governor, walker, confidante, counsellor, selfish middle-aged woman, home-manager.*

Apart from being a testament to the flexibility of human beings, the potential for conflicts of interest and needs is very evident.

Trainees experience, too, emotional intimacy within the course; the closeness and excitement of shared experiences is perhaps new to them and can exclude those at home. If they begin to change and grow in challenge to their old self, a sense of panic and conflict can become very hard to manage in their close relationships outside the course. We always remind intending course members that there can be costs as well as gains in counselling training – and one of the costs can be the stability of existing relationships. Equally, of course, the potential for self-knowledge and the opportunity to learn from feedback can allow people to grow in ways which deepen and enrich existing relationships. There are, though, very real risks – because there is such potential – in engaging in a process which, if it succeeds, will, by its very nature, promote change and growth.

Trainees can be helped by exploring frameworks which promote personal development and enable them to get a clear picture of the life space which accompanies them to the course, their valuing of it, what they might choose to change and what, if anything, is sacrosanct. There are many avenues into this, some discussed at more length in Chapters 7, 8 and 9. Two frameworks of particular value are the 'T formation' (Gilmore, 1973) and a 'people-in-systems' structure outlining the networks in which any individuals exist (Egan and Cowan, 1979).

The T formation is a model to enable someone to think through 'person –situation transactions', useful for a counsellor to help make sense of a client's world but helpful in training to apply to the trainee herself. Gilmore suggests that it is 'one vehicle for journeying towards self understanding' and a way of 'becoming familiar with ... the major themes and directions which are affecting someone at this point in his/her life'.

James, a Diploma student, drew a version of his life at the beginning of his course (see Figure 4.1).

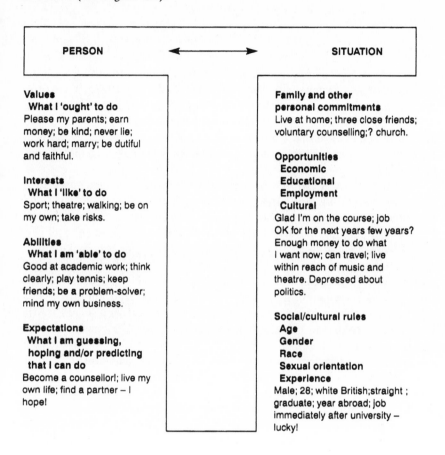

Figure 4.1 *The T formation (adapted by Gilmore, 1973)*

The T formation can be used to explore someone's present situation, by identifying past influences and messages about values and attitudes and can also be used to project forward, in terms of how someone might like to be, what she might want to work towards. Gilmore proposes developing the picture produced by marshalling self-knowledge in the T formation and then deepening self-understanding by relating it to the three main themes of life/counselling content, in her framework, of *work, relationship* and *aloneness*. Gilmore connects this process directly with the task of increasing self-acceptance, of 'prizing, valuing, affirming the significance of yourself as a complex and unique person'.

She outlines three aids to self-acceptance which the T formation can help to implement:

- Acknowledge personal limitations
- Acknowledge personal power
- Share yourself with other people.

Within 'the existential reality of being bound and limited by time and space and because human existence is absolutely bound by time which flows in one direction, every hour you choose to spend doing something with one person cannot be spent with someone else' (Gilmore, 1973). That pragmatic but honest injunction can be very helpful for trainees – or for any of us – prompted to review the significant elements and people in their lives and make choices about priorities, use of energy, and the relationship between their past, present and future and between counselling and the rest of life.

A similar process can be undertaken by adapting the concept of Egan and Cowan's (1979) people-in-systems model, by exploring in particular the interaction in values, attitudes, perceptions and pressures amongst the networks of personal settings and someone's wider social and cultural context. The essence of this is that we all exist in a range of personal contexts – family, friends, educational or work settings – all of which affect us and each other. These are in turn influenced by events in the broader institutions to which we cannot help belonging – the political, economic, media, religious and geographical worlds, which are themselves affected by the language, customs and changes happening in the broader culture of place and time in which we are all located.

Personal development involves much more than focusing on an individual trainee's immediate desires, needs and capacities. In my value system, it also involves relating all that to broader political and social concerns. Egan and Cowan's emphasis on the wider political life space and its implication is a very helpful stimulus in that direction and directly encourages people to see themselves – and their clients and their loved ones (or loathed ones!) – through many pairs of spectacles. And that again furthers the development of a personal and professional ability much needed by counsellors, reminding us that the focus of personal development, however valuable for the trainee's own life, must be in the service of counselling and clients. Not least then, in exploring life space issues that trainees bring, questions of oppression, of individual experiences of oppressing or being oppressed, may be very valuably explored. There are so many ways in which people can feel diminished and abused. In training groups I have known, participants have explored their lives as men and women, both, confusingly, feeling angry and less than valued; sexual, physical and emotional abuse have been shared and the pain and consequences re-felt and explored; all sorts of experiences of being 'outsiders' have been identified, for instance, being lesbian and homosexual, being black, having chosen childlessness, having a disability, especially a 'hidden' one , such as deafness or epilepsy, being strongly religious in a predominantly agnostic culture and so on. The opportunity to explore all this shared pain or abuse or powerlessness in the relatively safe environment of a course aids personal development, extends trainees' understanding and acceptance of themselves and others, and also triggers much potential learning about clients, their cultural and social contexts. The course itself and its relationships (see Chapter 6) may also parallel or re-stimulate responses to abuse or manipulation, since trainees are immersed in a very particular setting of power and influence. A Masters group, with whom I have worked, raised by its very composition and process many difficult but useful questions around gender and power. One woman member of the group reflected in a tutorial:

> *I've never before been in a group of so many strong women; although there are actually equal numbers of men and women, it feels as if there far more women present most of the time. What that does for me is make me feel sorry for the men – I want to rescue them so that they don't feel put down and dominated. So, I hide my own strength and skills and ability to lead ... and then I feel angry with the men and can sound really sharp with them!*

This strongly reminded her of the patterns in her own family, where the power struggle between her mother and father had never been resolved. Political attitudes towards gender issues were also often activated in that group, which inevitably raised questions of socialization and culture in the British society in which virtually all the group originated. Concerns about selection and the relatively homogeneous composition of many counselling courses are relevant here. Even if gender was in balance in that group, ethnic and other differences were minimal; hence missed opportunities for extending familiarity with a variety of life spaces and cultural contexts.

Transition

A third concept of value in identifying significant personal development issues for trainees is that of transition; its patterns and likely effects. Being on a course is in itself a transition from one state of knowing/doing/understanding to another; being in mid-life is another; changing roles, as some course members may be doing, from one work function to that of being a counsellor is yet another; and most of all, moving from being a competent, mature, averagely confident and coping adult to being an often anxious, insecure, about-to-be-assessed-adult learner, for many people is a truly enormous transition. The salient features of transition have been defined by various writers: Bridges (1933) described it as having three phases: (i) an ending, followed by (ii) a period of confusion and distress, leading to (iii) a new beginning. It inevitably means a loss of something, letting go of an aspect of life or self that matters, in order to move on to something else. Bridges describes a number of aspects of that losing, which, translated to a learning situation, trigger much personal exploration, in which awareness is high: disengagement, disidentification, disenchantment, disorientation. I can recognize versions of all of those if I let my mind scan back over students and trainees with whom I have worked (or learning situations in which I have been a student). So often, courses, even those where students have a great deal of control and self-direction, have the effect of deskilling people, especially where a degree of unlearning and of abandoning former perspectives on oneself are necessary. However willingly or reluctantly trainees engage with that process, there is a painful period of loss – and of being lost. In the learning model which suggests that we all move through four stages: *unconscious incompetence – conscious incompetence – conscious competence – unconscious competence* (Robinson, 1974), the most painful period for learners is in stages two and three which involve giving up a relatively secure self-image as a competent, successful person/practitioner. The loosening of those constructs, often tightly held like a comfort blanket, involves huge transitions for some trainees, but seems essential for well-based integrated new learning.

The other framework for understanding the effects of the kind of transition trainees experience is that based even more closely on theories of bereavement and grief. Most people, not all and not in the same order or degree, experience a series of emotional reactions until they can integrate their grieving (whether for a person or an aspect of themselves) and move on. The kind of stages generally described are: a kind of shock or numbness; followed by disbelief or denial; then a real sense of crisis, accompanied by anger or depression or both; a gradual acceptance of the reality of the loss; then a testing-out of new patterns and behaviours; followed by a searching for meaning and understanding; and finally, an integration of the experience, the loss and the new sense of self – with the ability, strength and desire to move on in whatever ways are appropriate. Key tasks in healthy coping with any kind of loss seem to involve acceptance, which may be gradual and painful, feeling the pain and not avoiding or minimising it, having enough flexibility to allow change in or outside oneself to happen and finding the willpower and energy to re-focus in whatever ways are necessary. It is obvious that while such processes are underway, individuals will feel vulnerable and possibly defensive, so may be less than easy in their relationships with others, may struggle to accept direction or feedback and are likely to be quite difficult group members! The implications for training and trainers are considerable, not least since every loss seems to bring up memories and unfinished business from every other loss of a similar or different kind. There are many aspects of being on a course in which trainees can experience different kinds of loss and related grief: as I suggested earlier, in changing perceptions of themselves; in re-evaluating other people's assessment of them; in reliving other learning situations which were painful attacks on self-confidence and competence; and in getting in touch with re-stimulated emotion connected with other actual life losses and bereavements of significant people, situations or relationships. A colleague recalled:

> *The first time I received critical feedback in a skills training session, I went home feeling really rubbished. Then suddenly, I found myself crying uncontrollably about my mother – she died five years ago. She sometimes had that capacity to make me feel stupid; as a child, I suppose I always hoped I'd be able to get it right one day – I think what was going on for me now was the sense that the chance had gone. I just felt so sad.*

The potential for – and indeed necessity of – personal work is clear, not least because many clients will also be experiencing aspects of loss which may trigger counsellors' own experiences of loss if they have not clarified and explored them.

At the same time as trainees are coping with a range of transitions internally, in the course, in their functioning as counsellors and as adult learners, ordinary human life flows on around them and through them. In an average counselling course group of sixteen to twenty-four mature adults, the number of expected and unexpected events or potential crises can be, indeed always is, enormous. Trainees are facing the pressures of the developmental tasks to do with ageing, families, work or career events, mid-life existential concerns; all the transition-related emotions and tasks I have just outlined; the joys and difficulties of being adult learners; and then, they individually – and the group collectively – may face bereavements, illness, accident, redundancy, relationship crises, financial pressures, unexpected good news and so on. In the first year of a course in which I was recently involved, the group members experienced for themselves or significant others in their lives – an adolescent child's schizophrenic breakdown; two road accidents; the death of three parents; two people made redundant; two affairs which split marriages; acceptance for emigration; house subsidence; a diagnosis of cancer; a stolen car; and a leg broken while skiing. Those were the experiences which were shared in the group or in tutorials and which triggered personal development material for everyone – including, of course, me the trainer – in different ways. There will of course have been other life experiences which were not directly part of the life of the group, but which will have been affecting individuals. Each of those shared or unshared experiences will have triggered major or minor transitions for both the individual concerned and for other group members. All this produces a wealth of material for personal development: the tasks are huge and infinitely complex for trainers in responding to those needs, while facilitating group reactions and process and managing purposeful progress towards the course objectives of training effective counsellors.

Working with clients

It is self-evident that a major impact on trainees, particularly if they have limited pre-course experience, will come from their interactions with clients. It is a course's responsibility, especially if BAC Recognised, to ensure that trainees have experience with a wide range of client ages, issues, and contexts, and, where possible, across gender and cultures. Any client can touch in the counsellor a nerve of unfinished business, can re-stimulate personal issues, present concerns and attitudes that shock, surprise, repel or seduce. Clients may, consciously or unconsciously, flood the counsellor with hostility, frighten her with deep depression, confuse her with flirtation, challenge her with intellectual or emotional games or frustrate her with lack of movement, progress or purpose. Supervision is the appropriate professional forum for intensive exploration of the process, strategies, techniques and safeguards relevant with any client; the counsellor's personal issues, feelings and concerns, whether directly triggered by the client or re-stimulated, countertransference responses, must be seen as core material for personal development, to be dealt with through all aspects of the course, as well as in trainees' own counselling/therapy. Fundamental human experience such as bereavement, sexuality, intimacy and distance, shame and guilt, life-threatening illness or self-loathing, family trauma or individual alienation and existential angst may all produce unexpectedly strong reactions in any counsellor, in training or not, which will need exploration and evaluation. The life-situations clients are in, perhaps facing bullying at work or discrimination because of who and what they are in colour, sexuality or religion, may again trigger anxieties, feelings or tensions in the counsellor. Very often with clients, it is the echo almost out of earshot, the faint stirrings of discomfort, the merest twinges of some feeling or thought on the edge of awareness, which counsellors have to learn to notice, capture gently like a butterfly, then examine, note, learn from and release for further development.

The shared experiences of a group of complex, mature adults facing a difficult though challenging and exciting task, produce in themselves almost unlimited personal development. The next chapter will consider ways of containing and focusing all this material, by providing some frameworks to enable proactive curriculum planning for personal development.

SOME QUESTIONS

1. Consider your own 'age and stage' and life space: how do they or would they affect you as a learner/counsellor/trainer?

2. What kind of losses might trainees experience during counselling training? How might they be balanced by gains?

3. Transition and bereavement have some similarities: what are the implications for counselling training?

4. Do you *believe* that you can always change because 'you can always learn new things'?

5. Is counselling training 'political' enough?

FIVE

What Stories can be Told?

Aims, objectives and themes: a curriculum for personal development?

The previous chapter outlined some frameworks for considering trainee personal development. It indicated the wealth of material available incidentally in any counselling training course. All those issues are likely to be present in different combinations and degrees of intensity. If the 'drama' of the course group is not to disintegrate into a screeching, cacophonous competition of strident and submerged voices, then a trainer needs some way of harnessing voices, energy and needs into a cooperative whole with space for everyone's issues. This chapter will argue that personal development in in-depth training courses should be proactive as well as reactive: it needs to be planned, at least as an outline, in addition to responding to what happens incidentally. This may seem a contradiction in terms: that something so individual, unique and personal can be identified and planned in advance – 'Here's one I prepared earlier' in the ubiquitous phrase from familiar television cookery programmes! It is not that every detail of the recipe and garnish for the trainee 'dish' should be planned; rather that the key ingredients, the fuel resources for cooking and the essential implements should be available in order that a sufficiently balanced 'meal' can be produced at the end of the process. So it is important that the trainer is clear what the aims and processes are, what stories the training group might need to cover and that she can hold that framework and ensure that the course provides appropriate triggers and opportunities for all voices. The detail of the 'script' and the specifics of the learning will then be improvised to greater and lesser degrees depending on the level and purpose of the course, the theoretical orientation, the experience and needs of the course members, indicated in this and the previous chapters.

It is important that trainers have some sense of what is essential, in order to monitor – if not assess (see Chapter 9) – trainee personal development. As a trainer, if you do not know what should or might be covered, what aspects of human experience can cause counsellors to stumble, how will you know what is missing in individual trainee development? Some examples follow of embryonic personal development programmes, based on different kinds of starting points: you might find it useful to develop your own thinking around each example.

(a) Outline the core aims expressed through a metaphor or image An image or metaphor can be a very helpful course planning device, conveying the essence of some key elements. Miller *et al.* (1975) posit a structure of development for relationships and communication, which can appropriately be applied to counselling. Their overall aim – and one underpinning, as Chapter 1 emphasized, all counselling training – is *awareness*: from this, they argue, can be identified all the elements necessary to build constructive human interaction. The starting-point for developing relevant understanding and skills is an 'awareness wheel' (Figure 5.1).

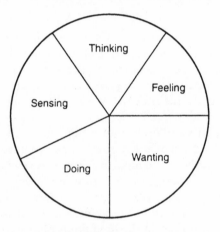

Figure 5.1 *Awareness wheel*

In each segment is a key area of awareness, which, fully developed, would make a substantial contribution to an effectively functioning person and/or counsellor. Each segment also influences all the others. The five areas for development – thinking, feeling, sensing, doing, wanting – when linked to counselling theory, ethical standards and skills are key in building a therapeutic relationship. To take one example: perhaps the most contentious area – and the one involving some of the complex in-depth questions of personal development – is that of *wanting*. For example: How do we want to see ourselves?; want others to see us?; how have we learnt to be covert and manipulative in what we want, especially in emotional areas?; what do we want out of counselling?; what is our motivation?; what needs/wants are being met?; what do we want from others, but don't say?; what influence, power, manipulation do we want over others?; how honest can we be with ourselves and others about what we want? and so on. What knowledge, exercises, feedback does any particular trainee need to explore these issues? Encouraging course members to design their own metaphor/image and tease out the learning elements, questions and processes is a valuable activity in any course of any length.

(b) Articulate the aims of counselling itself in any training and parallel them with the necessary personal development. For example, Hamblin (1974), in describing counselling with adolescents, emphasized these aims:

- fostering self-acceptance, not remediating personality;
- developing an internal locus of control;
- learning strategies and coping skills for situations which are difficult;
- developing decision making;
- understanding transitions;
- extending awareness of opportunities for growth and movement;
- understanding and coping with vulnerability, especially in crisis.

Those, if presented as core aims for a personal development course, cover quite a lot of ground! Think about the aims of any counselling you are engaged with: how might they translate into a personal development programme? What is missing?

(c) Make a detailed list of possible outcomes which trainees could/should experience as a result of change and development through their work on themselves. (Better still, encourage them to create their own list at the beginning, during and at the end of their training.) It should of course be a developmental and evolving list, rather than a fixed and prescriptive one. In an interesting article called 'Self-planned learning and major personal change' which has close parallels to counselling training. Tough (1976) outlines virtually a whole alphabet of possible outcomes:

WHAT PERSONAL CHANGES CAN SOMEONE STRIVE FOR?

a. self-understanding

b. express genuine feelings and interest

c. close, authentic relationships with others

d. broad understanding of history, geography, cultures, universe, future

e. better performance on the job; reshape the job or its meaning; new job

f.   quit drinking; stop beating children; quit heroin

g.   cope better with the tasks necessary for survival

h.   body free from excessive tenseness and wasted energy; physical fitness

i.   new priorities among goals (desired benefits); a fresh balance of activities or expenditures

j.   reshape relationship with partner; new partner; new circle of friends

k.   capacity for finding a calm centre of peace and inner strength amidst the turmoil

l.   adequate self-esteem

m.   reduction of psychological and emotional problems and blocks that inhibit full human functioning

n.   improved awareness and consciousness; more open-minded and inquiring; seeking an accurate picture of reality

o.   greater sensitivity to psychic phenomena and to alternate realities

p.   freedom, liberation, looseness, flexibility

q.   competence at psychological processing, at handling own feelings and personal problems

r.   zest for life; joy; happiness

s.   liberation from female-male stereotyping, or from other role-playing

t.   emotional maturity, positive mental health; higher level of psychological functioning

u.   spiritual insights; cosmic consciousness

v.   less selfish and more altruistic, a greater effort to contribute to the lives of others

w.   acceptance and love of self and others; accept the world as it is

x.   come to terms with own death

(Adapted from Tough, 1976, in Tight, 1983)

How does that compare with your possible list (or any counselling trainee's list) of desired or desirable outcomes? Some, such as (f) are perhaps (?) not relevant for most of us, but the greater part of Tough's list, if achieved, would certainly make me both a more complete person and a more effective counsellor and trainer!

(d) Design a framework for the whole training process and then extrapolate the personal development issues from that into a structured programme. Gilmore (1973) in her (North American) version of *The Counselor-in-Training* did exactly that, a very influential example for us when we developed one of the early integrated models of training at the then North East London Polytechnic in the 1970s.

Table 5.1 *Triadic structure (adapted from Gilmore, 1973)*

Content of counselling:	Work (Doing)	Relationship (Moving)	Aloneness (Being)
Purpose of counselling:	Choice	Change	Coherence (confusion/ reduction)
Process of counselling: Communicated through	Empathy	Acceptance	Genuineness
Nature of counselling:	Purposely-active	Social	Existential (Grappling with meaning/ uncertainty)

Gilmore's 'triadic structure' (see Table 5.1), translated through the experiences of small group work in a structured practicum (see Chapter 9), proved a powerful vehicle for personal and professional development, not least through the built-in links between theory, skills learning and feedback, and work on self. Gilmore's clarity too about the 'purposefully active' nature of counselling within both a social and existential reality, with the relationship's limited reciprocity and mutuality, limited time, place and involvement and its 'commitment to termination from the beginning' forcefully reminds us of the purpose of personal development as in the service of counselling.

(e) Outline (as concretely as possible) specific learning objectives for personal development and then design a range of activities to achieve and

assess them. Connor (1994) focuses on three areas: intrapersonal development, interpersonal development and attitudes and values. She outlines the learning objectives for each as follows:

INTRAPERSONAL DEVELOPMENT

Learning Objectives

1. To develop understanding and appreciation of self.

2. To become aware of and utilise personal strengths and assets.

3. To become aware of blind spots, blocks and vulnerabilities.

4. To identify areas to work on in personal counselling.

5. To appreciate experientially the significance of developmental stages in personal development.

INTERPERSONAL DEVELOPMENT

Learning Objectives

1. To understand areas of strength and areas for development in a range of interactions: with peers, staff, clients and in personal and professional relationships.

2. To gain confidence in appropriate self-sharing.

3. To develop skills of giving and receiving feedback.

4. To facilitate growth in self and others through active participation in personal development groups.

5. To develop helping relationships with clients.

6. To continuously reflect upon successes and setbacks and to use such reflection as the basis for setting realistic objectives for development.

7. To develop the internal supervisor, active not only during sessions with clients but also in other interactions whether group or individual.

ATTITUDES AND VALUES

Learning Objectives

1. To become aware of personal assumptions and beliefs.

2. To explore and clarify values and attitudes.

3. To develop core therapeutic qualities.

4. To be aware of ethical and professional issues and expectations in counselling.

5. To develop a personal code of professional ethics.

(Adapted from Connor, 1994)

Connor emphasises, as Gilmore does, that this part of the training process is designed 'to maximise opportunities for personal growth, but always at the service of clients' and not as 'an excuse for narcissistic absorption in self', a helpful reminder in terms of course design, balance and purpose. These objectives allow useful links to be made between theory and practice, self and clients, individuals and groups and encourage awareness and development primarily in the direction of flexibility: Connor quotes Whiteley *et al.* (1967) whose study demonstrated that counsellor effectiveness was linked positively to flexible construct systems. Flexibility is an interesting aim in itself, a key element in selection, though difficult to assess in personal development programmes.

(f) Identify key areas of competence around which training will be centred and then expand on how and when those elements will be taught/learned and what kind of evidence will be needed to demonstrate their achievement. McLeod (1993) offers 'a composite model', consisting of six distinct competence areas, namely: interpersonal skills; personal beliefs and attitudes; conceptual ability; personal 'soundness'; mastery of technique; ability to understand and work within social systems. The most relevant, in terms of personal development, are the areas of competence he describes as personal 'soundness' and personal beliefs and attitudes.

i) Personal 'soundness' is described as absence of personal needs or irrational beliefs which are destructive to counselling relationships, self-confidence, capacity to tolerate strong or uncomfortable feelings in relation to clients, secure personal boundaries, ability to be a client. Absence of social prejudice, ethnocentrism and authoritarianism

ii) Personal beliefs and attitudes involve capacity to accept others, belief in the potential for change, awareness of ethical and moral choices. Sensitivity to values held by client and self.

(McLeod, 1993)

Clearly, aspects of other competence areas have relevance too, especially interpersonal skills and ability to understand and work within social systems. The latter emphasises the needs for sensitivity to aspects of difference in other people, such as 'gender, ethnic, sexual orientation or age group' (McLeod, 1993). All six areas are interconnected, though with a different balance of perspective inwards, on the counsellor himself and outwards, on the client, theory or context. McLeod emphasises that during the counsellor's training journey – a developmental process – the quest must be for 'adequacy to task' and the constant question 'Am I good enough?' To be good enough, as McLeod says 'is to make a strong statement about one's own sanity, knowledge and competence' – taxing objectives indeed for personal development work!

Another example of a competency based outline is the work currently being developed in the field of NVQs (National Vocational Qualifications) through the efforts of the Lead Body for Advice, Guidance, Counselling and Psychotherapy, under headings such as:

- A5.2 Ensure continuing self development;
- B8 Monitor self within the counselling process;
- B8.1 Differentiate between own internal world and that of clients;
- B8.2 Monitor own effect on clients;
- B8.3 Ensure continuing self-support and supervision.
  (See *First Release of Standards*, National Vocational Qualifications, (1995), and later documentation)

The question challenging many trainers is whether a competency-based model of counselling or counsellor training is appropriate (necessary or sufficient?), particularly in the areas of personal development. Competency traditionally implies measurement, science not art, and it is generally agreed that other than the most general statement, little accurate measurement of counsellor effectiveness or of the person of the counsellor has yet been achieved.

(g) Finally, identify a central driving principle from which everything to do with personal development follows and by which individual outcomes are assessed. A useful example of a model such as this is Nelson-Jones' (1984) account called *Personal Responsibility Counselling and Therapy: An Integrative Approach*. Nelson-Jones defines personal responsibility as being at the heart of, indeed as the essence of, counselling and indeed of human living. Linked with Maslow's concept of self-actualizing, it consists of a continuous process in any individual of choosing and 'making' his or her life; Nelson-Jones argues that it leads to authenticity in relationships and a capacity to find meaning in activity and, if necessary, in suffering. It is, evidently, a philosophic view which places human life within existential parameters and in a constantly changing world; and validates the belief that people fashion their own lives, despite 'finitude and contingencies of fate' (Nelson-Jones, 1984). Its relevance as a framework for personal development could centre around these elements:

- Human beings are motivated by needs and fears yet want and seek higher order values such as altruism.
- Each individual is responsible for his or her own survival and fulfilment, which is a struggle since we are inherently fallible.
- Life involves validating or challenging our own self-conceptions and the ways in which we are defined by and define others.
- Feelings affect the making of choices.
- Thinking errors sustain distress.
- We need empathic relationships with other individuals and positive relationships in groups.

Each of those elements could provide considerable stimulus for a range of aspects of personal development, even if part of the struggle was to accept or diverge from the central philosophical tenets. Inevitably, an approach like this forces course members to explore directly their own beliefs and values, as well as being a springboard to examine facets of their intra- and interpersonal functioning.

Core elements

Those, then, are a number of ways of stimulating curriculum outlines for personal development, with which the particular structure, orientation, values, teaching/learning model, trainer style and course member needs and developmental stages will have to interact.

Rowan (1995) suggests a hierarchical progression of personal development in which he argues that different models of counselling fit the kinds of personal development possible at increasing levels of complexity. He sees the key elements of personal development as related to moral development, and particularly to psychospiritual development, a term taken from the work of Wilber (1990). Rowan's 'comparison of four positions in personal development' explores his suggested four stages of development, which he calls

- mental ego
- real self
- soul
- spirit

through comparisons of motivation, goals, processes, methods, helper roles, focus, basic statements, core questions and key issues.

The proposition has the merits of depth, detail, intellectual rigour and complexity; it is also rather impenetrable and not all to do with counselling, certainly in its ultimate emphasis on the spiritual quest and discipline of the fourth stage. It does however offer useful frameworks in definitions of the self in each developmental stage, models of counselling which Rowan sees as fitting into the aims and processes of each stage and differentiation (however contentious) amongst the challenges and issues of each stage. It is impossible to do justice here to the detail of Rowan's model, but the following extracted elements in Table 5.2 alone provide much food for thought for trainers in terms of personal development.

Table 5.2 Comparison of four positions in personal development (adapted from Rowan, 1995)

	i) Mental Ego	**ii) Real Self**	**iii) Soul**	**iv) Spirit**
Self	I am defined by others	I define who I am	I am defined by the other(s)	No definition
Motivation	Need	Choice	Allowing	Surrender
Process	Healing	Development	Opening	Enlightenment
Key Questions	Dare you face the challenge of the unconscious?	Dare you face the challenge of freedom?	Dare you face the loss of your boundaries?	Dare you face the loss of all your symbols?

Finally in this section, what is *my* minimum outline for personal development in counsellor training? Any programme should work for awareness and acceptance and enable individuals to work towards the following objectives:

- To learn and unlearn.
- To have enough sense of identity to survive and flourish in personal and professional relationships.
- To love and be loved enough.
- To have sufficient self-esteem and personal power to cope with dependence, independence and interdependence.
- To be resourceful and creative.
- To notice and oppose oppression in whatever form it comes.
- To be strong and vulnerable, tough and tender as needed.
- To understand and apply theory and skills relevantly to themselves and others.
- To grow in clarity about ethical standards and never be complacent.
- To be aware of their own and others' needs for support and challenge.
- To have a range of effective ways of being alone and in a group.
- To see and feel connections with a wider society and world; to be political and care about change, however they live that out.

Since such an outline must be formative, developmental and, like trainee counsellors, constantly in the process of change, on a different day, month, year, I will have a different list! I am aware, too, that these elements are not all simple and uncontentious.

This chapter has considered some possible approaches for planning a curriculum for personal development; the next chapter will explore the other essential elements: the trainers and the course itself.

SOME QUESTIONS

1 Is a 'personal development curriculum' a contradiction in terms for you?

2 What would be your starting points and essential elements, if you were designing such a framework?

3 Do counsellors – and counsellor trainers – need 'personal soundness'? (McLeod, 1993). What is it?

4 Take Rowan's four 'Key Questions': what would be the implications of each of them for you?

SIX

Holding the ring or pulling the strings?

Trainers and their courses: What do they contribute to personal development?

Other than in specifically self-help groups, all trainees are partnered in their complex learning dance by trainers, tutors, facilitators, however described, and the nature, style, orientation and quality of the course they run. The BAC *Code of Ethics and Practice for Trainers* (1994) stresses that trainers must operate with 'integrity, impartiality and respect' with an 'appropriate use of self'. Those of us who are trainers, work, we hope, constantly towards that aim and standard. We must acknowledge, though, that this is difficult. In any moment of exchange with a trainee or a group, there is a need for fine judgement, sensitive awareness, knowledge of our own strengths and our shadow, together with our empathy for and valuing of the other person: as Hamblin (1974) said of counselling itself, 'No easy task'.

TRAINERS

Connor (1994), '... in counselling training there is nowhere to hide', has outlined how pressured and stressful counselling training can be, what demands there are on trainers and what it means to be a 'good enough trainer'. Mearns (Mearns and Thorne, 1988) says in terms of person-centred counsellor training, that 'its true challenge is the enormous personal development work which is necessary to win a sufficient degree of self-acceptance which will allow the counsellor to feel consistently unthreatened, accepting and open to the experience of her clients'. If that is true for counsellors in training, it is certainly true of their trainers: exchange the word trainer for counsellor and trainees for clients and the extent and nature of the task for trainers begins to be clear. Counselling trainers will be experiencing the direct and indirect effect of trainees' life-stages, life spaces, crises and transitions – as well, of course, their own.

Becoming a trainer has many elements:

- Understanding and applying theory and the implications for training of one's own theoretical orientation.
- Being a competent practitioner who can teach, model and give accurate feedback about counselling skills.
- Having some clarity of conceptual thinking and effective communication skills to convey ideas and capture processes.
- Being knowledgeable and competent in practical organization, ensuring resources, structuring time.
- Having sufficient experience of course design and teaching and learning models to tailor a course appropriately for its level of qualification, the needs of the group and 'the many masters' of an institution, a validating body, BAC, the counselling world, the needs of clients and so on.

All of those have an effect on and are influenced by the person of the trainer. This chapter will focus on some further specific areas which have particular implications for the trainer and her personal development. These include:

- Awareness of the range of training roles, styles and interventions and their effects.
- The nature of the demands on a trainer; the resources a trainer must have to meet them; her own needs.
- The 'Janus' position (facing two ways at once) of the trainer, at the interface between trainees and an organization/institution.
- Issues of responsibility and power, in particular of being, in effect, a change agent in others' lives.
- Managing the paradox of needing considerable confidence and self-belief to be an effective trainer, yet retaining a core sense of humility, fallibility and vulnerability to avoid hubris (excessive pride!), stay human and survive!
- Communicating the core qualities of empathy, genuineness and acceptance: making them available in relationship with trainees so that you-the-trainer and you-the-person are one, within ethical, personal, theoretical, philosophical and values boundaries?
- Understanding the potential of different philosophies of training, the implications for course design and the learning needs of the trainer herself.

Roles, styles and interventions: power and responsibility

Trainers and trainees can function, in the duration of any course, in a range of roles. Some of the most interesting work on roles, particularly in terms of the power they can command, has been developed by Brigid Proctor

(1991). Based on the notion of archetypes, which reflect some kind of universal meaning over time and cultures, a role is a way of operating, a functional activity which enables something else to happen; roles involve flexibility and creativity, and suggest a range of possible functions or 'ways of doing.' That a trainer should be effective in any number of role behaviours might seem incompatible with the concept of core qualities, 'ways of being', especially genuineness, touched on in the previous section. They rather allow a trainer, however centred, clear and grounded, to operate with flexibility, through a variety of functions and activities. Archetypes can, too, often be projections, allowing people to be in our eyes what we consciously or unconsciously want them to be. In other ways, they can also enable any of us to exercise parts of our personalities which reflect the way we most want to be seen by others or parts which we are not sure of or do not much like. In training, archetypes also reflect activities, captured in metaphor, which have to be undertaken by trainers and trainees.

Proctor's archetypes in the training context include the Patriarch, who creates order and unselfconsciously wields power; the Guru or Wise Woman from whom wisdom is expected; the Earth Mother, all providing, accepting, prizing; the Clown or Jester, enjoying performance, being clever; the Actor/Director who holds the ring, has an overview, with some control, and organizes others into roles and tasks; the Bureaucrat who insists on being concrete and on boundaries and obedience to rules; the Whore (in a strictly trainer sense) who loves group after group – and lets them go – while being paid for her services; the Warrior, seeking and fighting for truth; the Judge who is objective, and impartial, assessing standards; the Shepherd and Sheep Dog, who keep everyone safe and rounded up; and the Communicator who is open and real and talks clearly about what is happening. In terms of any individual trainer's personal development, a useful task may be to identify roles which are not comfortable or spontaneous and explore the internal messages and blocks to operating in those ways. Similarly, it may be productive to focus on the roles that seem to come naturally and question what the reward is or what personal history/experience has nudged those patterns into operation. From my own experience, for example:

> *In earlier years as a trainer, I found being Earth Mother enticing and very satisfying, but sometimes had to silence my Warrior. I have always been resistant to and uncomfortable in being Judge, yet my Bureaucrat knows the Judge's value and reminds me of his importance – and that I can be 'him' well and with integrity. Now, I actively want to avoid being Wise Woman, have given away (too soon perhaps) much of my Clown and feel, slightly reluctantly, much more comfortable with being Actor/Director and even at times Patriarch. Being Whore, feels both easier – I think I have less need for emotional investment in the moment – and more difficult – harder, with each course, to find the energy to engage at depth.*

Power

In all this, a central issue for trainers is our relationship with power, control and influence; how honest we can be about the kind of power we enjoy or avoid or deny; how invested we are, as Heron (1990) has expressed it, in 'power over/power shared with/facilitation of power within'; and how willing we are to receive feedback on our patterns of exercising power. There are many frameworks for exploring this issue, not least Heron's analysis of the kinds of interventions we have at our disposal and how we choose to use them and for what effect. For instance, in personal development work in particular, he suggests that we are more likely to be 'cathartic, catalytic or supportive'. There is of course power in all of those modes, but it is different in effect – and perhaps less honest – than interventions which are 'prescriptive, informative or confronting' (Heron, 1990), which exercise power more directly and openly.

Other useful models for exploring the dynamics of power are the Parent-Adult-Child framework from transactional analysis (Byrne, 1972); the Karpman Triangle (1968) of victim-rescuer-persecutor; and the concept of games as outlined by Goffman (1961), (all quoted by Connor, 1994). Power, in training, as in life, is generally thought of as not desirable, yet as Rogers (1978) emphasised, 'I want very much to have influence and impact … '. The reality of social existence and counselling training is that issues of power, powerful, powerless, power over, power-from-within, disempowered and empowering are unavoidable. The challenge for us as trainers is to face, identify and learn to use constructively all the power play, power issues and power tensions which, consciously or unconsciously, will be enmeshing us with any individual, group, course or organization within which we work. Speedy (1993) has constructed a meta-theoretical model of power, with particular attention to gender, which allows for 'authority and domination as well as flexibility and transformation' in its application to counselling training. She explores the different difficulties for men and women counselling trainers, within the social constructions of gender and power, in balancing the demands of offering support and challenge, the implicit power in the trainer role and the values of counselling around empowering. Speedy posits that just as women seem to use language differently (and be described in different language than men), so they may also have a 'different moral identity that draws them towards different notions of powerfulness', possibly linking power less with status and authority than with influence and energy. This is a complex issue, clouded by social expectations, cultural influences, self-concept, needs for approval and all kinds of earlier family, societal and educational influences: many people's first experience of a power/authority figure outside the home is of their first (almost invariably female) teacher at infants school. The shadows of that experience hover uneasily in many a training room, affecting trainees' attitudes to trainers (especially female ones) and triggering shifting patterns of transference and counter-transference. When I've asked trainees to exaggerate, for exploration, their picture of 'the ideal trainer', an impressively powerful figure emerges:

> *She will be all-knowing, all-seeing, all-understanding; she will appreciate all my difficulties in the course without my needing to say anything about them; she'll have infinite time, patience and resources; she will never show moodiness, favouritism or pettiness, never be unfair, get anything wrong or have any visible needs of her own. She won't expect me to take any responsibility (or will give me unquestioned responsibility!). She will have a sense of humour, look beautiful and always be kind. She'll know every academic reference, be brilliant – always! – at counselling and supervision. And she will never be ill!*

Even if we disallow most of that fantasy hybrid of Miss Jean Brody and Florence Nightingale, there is enormous power in the role of trainer, both directly in most courses, in terms of selection, structure, assessment, the giving of references and so on and indirectly, in terms of the possibilities for abuse and oppression, emotional, sexual or professional manipulation. Most exploitation occurs due to 'a combination of inadequate self-awareness and supervision, theoretical, ethical and practical incompetence and abuse of the helper/helped (read trainer/trainee) power relationship' (Bond, 1993). For all these reasons, the imperative is strong for trainers to continue to work with their own personal development to identify desires, distortions in perception, antipathies, motivations and reluctances – or evasions, avoidances, blind spots and needs which should be met elsewhere. It is important to acknowledge the seductiveness of being a trainer, in terms of personal satisfactions – the adrenaline of surfing the wave of group experience; the warm glow of creative tutorial exchanges; the (parental?) delight of seeing trainee counsellors grow and flourish as independent professionals and competent 'helpers'; and the pleasure in ending a well-managed course, of letting it and the group members go ... and feeling relief! That somewhat orgasmic-sounding process must be owned as pleasurable and rewarding, but must not be primarily in the trainer's interest nor a principal means of meeting her needs. With adult learners, it is unhelpful and inappropriate to be paternalistic. It is important, in contrast, honestly to admit the pressures and pleasures of a kind of parental power, inevitable in controlling resources, having overall direction of a course and the group, which is yet ethically limited. It is helpful to accept those realities and the power suggested by 'social influence theory'. (Strong, 1968) This suggests that if a trainer/counsellor/helper is perceived as expert, attractive and trustworthy, then he or she inevitably has the potential for disproportionate power over the trainee/client, which must be acknowledged and worked through. If not, the seductive nature of the relationship is unhealthy and unhelpful. Even in courses at the extremes of the self-directed/student-centred continuum, when trainers' commitment is to move as far away from the power-holding, parental position as possible, these are still live issues and trainers ignore them at their – or their trainees' – peril.

As Thorne (1987) put it, trainers must listen to 'the changing and probably chaotic flow of experience taking place within themselves. It is exhausting and demanding work'. It is even more so if the concept of trainer power includes positive transformational energy.

Responsibility

It may be helpful to understand power as less the ability to control, but rather as the capacity to effect change. The other side of the gift of power (since it is then a gift) is that accompanying it must come responsibility – for self and others. A key part of a trainer's personal development is balancing those responsibilities.

Responsibility to self. I notice as I write that I want to begin by exploring first responsibilities to others: that reflects my own tendency, at times, as a trainer, to give less than adequate attention to my own needs. In my younger days as a trainer, I think on some level I saw that as dutiful, part of commitment, certainly seductive and possibly heroic in some subliminal way. I have come to recognize that it is counter-productive, inefficient, at times sacrificial and ultimately leads to less effective work – the whole becomes less than the sum of the parts. Fatigue, burn-out, the death of creativity and personal energy loom as very real dangers. So, trainers beware! Let me begin instead with responsibility to self – to be clear about the ways in which we drain and replenish our resources; pay attention to our needs; and ensure our fitness, in all senses, to be trainers and human beings. Egan (1986) suggests the notion of the 'ideal helper': while this may give us an ambitious model to work towards, it may be an unrealistic and even unhelpful notion. The concept of being 'a good enough helper/trainer' may be more valuable (Connor, 1994).

Dainow and Bailey (1988) suggest seven internal resources for power, confidence and strength: self-esteem, knowledge, communication, affection, passion, control, and transcendence (the last translated as knowing when to rise above what cannot be controlled or changed). Trainers might usefully explore on a regular basis whether they are high or low on each of those elements and what they need in order to compensate for the deficiencies. The same writers also remind us of the framework based in Transactional Analysis of the 'five drivers', the automatic patterns of thinking, feeling and acting which we fall into particularly at times of stress. The drivers – Be Perfect, Please, Try Hard, Be Strong and Hurry Up – have been internalized in childhood, in individual patterns and hierarchies, as 'survival rules'. Each tends to produce patterns of feeling and behaviours which may be counter-productive both for the trainer and certainly for her trainees! As Dainow and Bailey emphasize, working on awareness of the five drivers implies 'the willingness to accept responsibility for engaging in change that may mean long term effort'. For everyone involved in counselling training, that certainly seems a central concept.

A further useful framework against which trainers might measure themselves in terms of self-responsibility, is Gilmore's (1984) 'S' model. She proposes that any helper, counsellor, manager or trainer, involved in interpersonal interactions needs to engage systematically and over time with a continuous audit of these five areas which in her view include the essentials for living and working effectively:

> Situation   Style   Skills   Stamina   Spirit

Gilmore also describes these as:

> Circumstances   Competencies   Character   Fitness   Faith
> *or*
> Context   Tools   Temperament   Toughness   Transpersonal.

It is a salutary process for any trainer to define those terms for herself, evaluate her strengths and limitations at any particular point of development and identify needs, resources and supports. It is significant, too, to relate any evaluation of those aspects with changes (as for trainees) of life space and age and stage. If I do that task now, I notice some significant differences from ten years ago, just before I began my present job, which was to develop a counselling programme at the University of Bristol.

> *My commitment and passion for the work (spirit) are not diminished; my working context is more supportive and better-resourced in some ways and less consistent and caring in others. My ability to work in a wider range of training styles and roles has increased (I have strengthened reflective facilitation and offer less of the all-singing, all-dancing actor-teacher, a kind of 'performing seal' – though I can still do that!). As my day-to-day responsibilities have moved more to the management and supervision of a very large course programme, I have lost, I think, an edge of ability in some skills which I felt particularly good at, such as working with trainees in an effective way with video, but improved in others, such as supervision. I feel much wiser, if less knowing, and much less absolute in my views, though more confident; and I certainly feel older, more tired, recover from effort less quickly and begin to envy the energy of those rather earlier in their training careers!*

All trainers must take responsibility for finding supports and resources outside themselves to help replenish what training (and life – both demanding activities!) drain away. Supervision, personal counselling, peer support, close colleagues, old friends (especially those who are also old trainers), my partner and family, animals, music, books and nature, food and drink, all in their different ways at different times are crucial for me. I resolve every year to be clearer about my own needs, to put responsibility for *me* higher up my list of priorities – and I think I am getting better at it, though slowly.

Responsibility to others. Counselling training never takes place in a vacuum. Most trainers operate within some kind of organization or institutional context which demands from them responsibility and accountability for functions such as budgeting, staff management, resource organization, institutional involvement in committees or working parties, or public relations with outside bodies who have power or influence. If the organization is one for which the trainers hold some power and control, such as in a private firm, then the demand, in terms of responsibility will be for consistency of values in the operation of all activities, for managing the context, the administration, the nuts and bolts, in ways which match the stated values of the courses. If in contrast, a course and its trainers operate within an organization which runs on different values, the trainer has a still more complex task. Some counselling courses in higher education, for example, face many tensions in matching resource and staffing needs, the style of assessment and the nature of relationships with the traditional expectations of formal institutions. Experienced trainers who hold senior posts in those settings have to manage, Janus-like, to face in two directions. They must attempt to meet trainee needs and demands in ways consistent with the values of counselling, while fighting for resources and maintaining their own role of influence and responsibility in a context where values may be very different. This has dangers of creating considerable dissonance and an ultimate testing of personal integrity. Within a course, there is a danger of trainers promoting 'splitting' – course good, institution bad, an unhealthy position, though often very tempting. This reflects many contexts where counselling itself is an uneasy fit; there are thus considerable demands on trainers to identify their own personal issues, manage their feelings and work openly to resolve conflict, both internal and external – and make sure they have appropriate consultative support and supervision outside the organization, especially (but not only) if there is insufficient support within it.

Responsibility to co-tutors. The fluid boundary between personal and professional development comes into focus where responsibility to others involves co-tutoring, being a member of or leading a team of tutors. Assagioli's (1975) concept of 'right relations' is central, with its potential for managing tensions and paradoxes and promoting cooperation and valuing, yet is often a tall order. Most trainers (and most training organizations such as BAC and RSA) accept that co-tutoring is more desirable, more effective and more productive of learning, especially at a substantial course level; any of us who do it experience its joys and rewards and its occasional experiences of hurt or pain. All the advantages of co-leading courses and working in teams can only be available if trainers work on themselves and between themselves for openness, trust and means of resolving conflicts and differences which must arise with two or more human beings working closely under pressure or stress. Rivalry, competition, status, promotion, control, need-to-be-loved-by-trainees issues, knowing-best battles, likes and dislikes, self-esteem panics may all be in-the-moment reactions, plus all the shadows of family and sibling discomforts, parent–child dynamics, friendships, failed and successful intimate relationships from the past and our whole living, loving, learning and working histories! In addition to all that trainers *bring*, individual trainees, co-trainers, groups and institutions will also *send* roles, reputations, comparisons, family and other messages: it is an understatement to suggest that there may be much to work on in this area in trainer personal development. It must also be said that, at times, all of those issues, feelings and responses have to be noted, but suspended, since more immediate tasks have to be done: timing and the ability to judge appropriateness are significant skills, at least as important for trainers as counsellors. It is a fine judgement as to when, for example, an emotion, difficulty, issue or conflict between trainers should be dealt with there-and-then because it is impeding the work of the course and group; or acknowledged and logged, then taken elsewhere – to supervision, consultancy or peer-exchange – to be dealt with in open exploration. As Levine (1980) stresses 'it is folly to hold a group back for the sake of the learning of the co-leaders!'

Responsibility to the world of counselling. Finally, in terms of responsibility to others, trainers also have some need to consider whether and how they engage in the wider world of counselling, in BAC, in committees and working parties, in regional organizations, as an external examiner or consultant to other developing courses or organizations, writing books and articles, and so on. Spinning the roundabout of experience and exchanging ideas between individuals and organizations can only be valuable. Sometimes, though, personal status in the larger, counselling world becomes more important than the home base and humdrum responsibilities. Self-monitoring of needs and motivations must be a key element in any trainer's personal work: noticing how the balance of needs changes over time; weighing altruism with selfishness, public image with private tasks. This may parallel for the trainer the counsellor's duty (and sometimes struggle) to keep the client's (trainees') needs in primary focus. As so often, the response to such questions centres on balance – of self and others' needs, of disseminating experience yet maintaining priorities; of feeding oneself by undertaking different activities yet sustaining the core, central responsibilities. That balance is sometimes hard to keep – and it changes imperceptibly over time.

Responsibilities to trainees. Trainers have a particular responsibility, since they are almost always operating as change-agents in the lives of trainees. All the potential learning, whether of theory, skills, attitude and perceptions is bound to have effects on the trainee as a human being as well as a counsellor. The 'unintended consequences' of training events and relationships may be as significant as planned interventions; and planned processes have a way of changing direction, purpose or effect 'on the hoof'. It is essential, for the sake of trainees, that trainers continue to work on their own personal development, in order to increase awareness, identify their own patterns and blind spots, and be consistently as clear as possible in thoughts and feelings about their motivation, needs and intentions.

The trainer is, in effect, a catalyst for change, alongside all the other choices, relationships and life events which will also be operating for the trainee. Clark (1991), however, argues that the usual understanding of catalyst – something that exerts a force on something else, thereby effecting change without being changed itself – may be appropriate for traditional models of training, but is at odds in training exchanges built around the helping relationship qualities of understanding, acceptance and genuineness. He redefines the trainer as change-agent into a *process* of working with the trainee to manage jointly the cycles of learning and whatever changes result. The relationship has, in addition to a high measure of the core qualities, the following elements:

- the trainer is also a learner about the trainee, their interaction and the trainee's effect on her;
- the process is interactive, in that both are open to change and new awareness;
- the trainer, while being fully engaged and not judgemental, operates both as reflecting mirror – this is what I see and notice, and as a licensed idiot questioning the obvious.

All of this asks a great deal of a counsellor trainer, but reflects a reciprocal commitment to that of the trainee. The challenge in terms of trainer personal development is to negotiate a position between wearing expertise lightly, yet not be locked into being the expert; having status and authority, yet work for equality of value and willingness in the training relationship; make judgements about the professional competence of trainees but avoid being either judgemental or unknowingly over-influential.

As Clark emphasizes, to learn and change requires willingness, trust and support in ourselves and those around us. However high the value placed on this in counselling training, apart from all those who survive and flourish, whatever the challenges, there will be some trainees who will not be ready or able to embark on the process. Trainers then have a difficult responsibility: any training programme will have expectations and standards of movement in the direction of certain kinds of change and yet all individual trainees, having been accepted onto a course, also have rights, needs and expectations of support. The concept of the 'teachable moment' Rogers (1986), is relevant; and resistance to learning, as Clark reminds us, can be defined as a protection against the dangers of learning and change. A crucial element of any trainer's work on herself will be to examine her own responses to negative or resistant attitudes in course members, to work for an understanding of those attitudes and to find acceptable ways of working with, around or towards the trainee's unwillingness to learn, in supervision, tutorials and personal development work. A degree of self challenge may be relevant here, to any trainer's fundamental philosophy about learning and training:

- Do you believe that people learn better when supported, accepted and held in a warm climate?
- Do you believe, that in order to learn, people have to face discomfort, be pushed through resistance and have anxiety increased?
- Do you believe that a balance of those two modes is necessary?
- If so, what are your limits? How much anxiety is too much? What degree of resistance is acceptable/too costly?

All of these questions involve a trainer's professional development and are appropriate for supervision. The personal development implications in particular may be around servicing our own unresolved issues or past experiences as trainers and trainees; identifying any emotional loading from our own history which we bring to the training dilemmas involved; and untangling our own needs, hurts or wants in the ways in which we read or respond to trainee difficulties – or indeed to difficult trainees. For instance, a relatively experienced trainer brought to supervision the following concern:

> *I am getting so irritated with Ben in the new Diploma group. He seems to feel he has to question everything at great length, even the simplest instruction. When I can stand back from the process, I can see that partly he is anxious and partly that is what he thinks an adult student is supposed to do! In the moment though, I am beginning to feel that I want to be really sarcastic to him, just to shut him up.*

When she continued to explore that situation, it became clear that as well as the legitimate concern about the appropriateness of Ben's behaviour, there was an inappropriateness in the degree of her response which stemmed from an early experience as a trainer. She had felt quite helpless in her first training course, when an older man had (rightly) challenged the accuracy of a position she had taken. Her confidence had been shaken, and although it all felt a long time ago, Ben was in some way re-stimulating some core lack of belief in herself. This clashed uncomfortably with her trainer values of accepting and supporting trainees and was producing dissonance and discomfort.

Not all responsibility, of course, belongs to the trainer: some trainees *are* difficult, with their own agendas, bent on subverting or sabotaging perfectly adequate, indeed creative course content and process and trainer behaviour. Trainer responsibility then, in terms of our own development, is to work for the awareness, knowledge and skills to challenge appropriately those course members who are potentially destructive or even just consistently oppositional. Most of all, perhaps, we must be clear about who and what frightens us, how we handle fear, what frightening figures in our own lives we are often reminded of, and how we can strengthen our own resolve and grow in courage. Almost to my own surprise, courage is somewhere high on my list of trainer needs, as part of executing our responsibility to others. In addition to dealing with 'difficult group members', courage is also needed to identify people at risk, people who are not ready, too needy, too raw, too frightened to change or too unhealthy in any sense to cope with the pressures of counselling training. They may, of course, in any particular moment, be trainees, fellow-trainers or even me – or you!

There are many aspects to the roles and functions, power and responsibilities of being a trainer. It is well to remember in Connor's (1994) words, that trainers and trainees are 'both robust and vulnerable'; there is an almost infinite loop of issues, awarenesses, insights and feelings on which to work, if, as trainers we take seriously our own professional and personal development.

Training philosophy and functions

I am a teacher: trainers who are not teachers start from a different position, but all must question their underlying assumptions, values and attitudes towards learners and learning, the essential context of all that has preceded this section. Those attitudes are not always easy to surface, buried as they may be under the volcanic flow of our own educational experiences, our contacts with education as consumers, parents or citizens, our confusion or clarity over rights and responsibilities, authority and authority-figures and our own fears and aspirations. There is a central paradox: that adult learners need different learning possibilities than children have traditionally (if wrongly and inadequately) been given, yet, placed in a new learning context, adults often behave like children! Treading a clear and safe path is then difficult for the trainer, between the extremes of too-directed, tightly-structured courses and disorganized, unfocused chaos. The continuum from tutor-directed teaching to student/self-directed learning is a winding path, fraught with dangers, if enlivened with excitements.

Trainers do have to decide whether they see themselves primarily as educators, facilitators, or task-focused leaders; whether they see adult trainees/students/learners as relatively empty vessels to be filled by traditional jug-pouring-into-mug didactic teaching or as independent minds, bringing valuable experience, with the right to choose, plan and design their own learning, within appropriate other-or-self-defined goals; whether their (the trainers') responsibility is primarily content, process or boundary keeping, and so on. The reality, of course, is that these should not be either/or: at different times in different courses all will be relevant. The 'ought' for trainers is the process of thinking through those issues, understanding the implications of each of them and then matching the outcomes to both trainee and trainer experience, style and learning/training needs. A trainer I worked with some time ago offered the following thoughts:

> *Five years ago, I thought I knew what I was doing; I knew I was competent; I could plan, structure, time and manage courses really well and felt very much in control. I think that is all still true, but I began to feel less-than-honest in teaching very directively the values in counselling, which were all about autonomy and shared responsibility and cooperative working. This inconsistency has pushed me further towards negotiated learning. It feels harder to do well. but more right and appropriate.*

Just as the centrality of the working relationship has been accepted in virtually all models of counselling, so in training. Whatever the theoretical orientation of the trainer, there is general agreement that the ability to communicate the core qualities of empathy, genuineness and acceptance is key in creating an effective working relationship. Indeed Combs (1986) argued that all effective counsellor education should be essentially person-centred, in order to be congruent with the aims of counselling itself. Combs also emphasized that the core of such training should enable trainees to explore in depth their belief systems, in order to achieve a 'trustworthy belief system' that gives them ways of perceiving and making sense of the world which are 'comprehensive, accurate, internally congruent, personally relevant, and continuously adaptable to modification as required'. From this will follow all other learning, of behaviour and skills, of theory and practice, with 'authenticity and personal fit' highly likely, led by a sense of need to learn and commitment to the learning process. If this is true for trainees, then the same process of clarifying belief systems must also be essential for counselling trainers; it will drive their choice of teaching aims and their understanding of the functions they can fulfil. This person-centred training model is attractive and makes sense to me, yet I must accept that trainers whose theoretical counselling orientation is different may well find some incongruity between the essence of the values in this approach and some of their own given frameworks and concepts. Just as, in counselling, for some people the core qualities are 'necessary but not sufficient', so trainers will need to add the elements significant in providing an integrated match between their training model and their theory. Psychodynamically orientated trainers, for example, are likely to consider how issues of containment and boundaries of different kinds operate in their course; cognitive-behavioural trainers might want to monitor, in particular, the integration of structured learning activities and models of effective and dysfunctional thinking. The 'right' balance of feeling, thought and action will be different for every trainer, depending on her values, philosophy and orientation; matching that to the needs of trainees through appropriate adult-to-adult relationships in joint purposeful endeavour is the central training task. A trainer's personal development involves surfacing, exploring and finding ways of using constructively her ease/dis-ease in different modes and learning to be as flexible and responsive as possible. Trainers may also need to learn to be invisible. I have often been aware that some of my best training (and the trainees' best learning) has been done in courses where the feedback has hardly mentioned me! It has taken me some years of experience, though, actively to enjoy this and recognize with Rogers (1983) that 'the rewards of an excellent facilitator are different from the rewards of a brilliant teacher'.

Trainers, then, need some understanding about the continuum of learning positions, the movement from dependent students to self-directed learners; a continuum which ranges from an entirely trainer-centred and directed course to a student-centred, self-directed course. A crucial task for any trainer is to match those positions with her own style, qualities, needs and resources. Grow (1991) developed a 'staged self-directed learning' model which explores the match between student needs and trainer style; he emphasises that trainees may need to move at their own pace from a first stage which is likely to be dependent to a later stage of capacity for independent and more self-directed learning. Grow proposes the useful notion of match and mismatch between learner stages and trainer styles: when they are most at odds, relationships are least effective and learning impaired. For example, when a trainer committed to self-directed learning is faced with students who lack confidence or skills and who are consequently very dependent, they may see each other very negatively. The trainer's tasks are to have a range of approaches available to her, to be clear what sits congruently and what uneasily for her and any trainee group and to work to own and use the differences. Co-training – advocated anyway for large or in-depth groups – is often a helpful and enlightening arrangement, when colleagues need to share enough values and belief systems genuinely to work cooperatively, yet can have different styles, strengths and patterns of response to students. It is not, though, always an easy option! (see 'Responsibility to others', earlier in this chapter.)

As Rogers (1983) stressed in his general exploration of educational methods, the central shift in being a trainer of counsellors is from teacher to facilitator, 'holding the attitude and possessed of the skills of ... genuineness, prizing and valuing'. The implications are profound for trainers who accept this view and those values. It is not possible to be a facilitator with adults, which demands cooperation, equality of valuing and status (if difference of function), openness and realness of self *and* be protected by role distance, hidden behind status, and disguised by lack of self sharing. This view again might be harder to accept for trainers from different orientations. As Rogers emphasizes, too, desirable though this may be, it involves a great deal of personal risk and vulnerability: if I am to be real, I cannot be 'perfect'. This can be costly for me, for example, with my own 'Be Perfect' and 'Try Hard' drivers, but it can also be difficult for trainees, some of whom, like adolescents, need me to be perfect, so that they can either love me or loathe me – or both! Each trainer will have her own version of this dilemma! As an experienced trainer, I am convinced that of Rogers' three qualities, it is genuineness which is the most challenging, with its truly difficult skills of immediacy and self disclosure. As trainers, we sometimes talk rather glibly of learning and using those skills, casually dropping in phrases such as 'appropriately timed' and 'the needs of the trainee'. The reality is that to use such skills and be consistently genuine over time is enormously difficult, with a range of trainees and throughout whatever personal and professional events are happening. Inevitably, the process produces a great deal of raw material for trainer personal development, whether it is then taken to personal counselling, supervision, peer exchange with co-trainers or reflected on alone. And ultimately, as a trainer, in the moment, one is alone and can feel very lonely.

THE COURSE ITSELF

In any counselling course, key elements are the nature of the learning group; the 'critical incidents' throughout the life of a course; the balancing acts which all members of the course community have to manage; and the models for personal and professional growth consistently offered by all aspects of the course and the training experience; and especially the trainers, their philosophy of training and the climate they desire and are able to create.

Teaching and learning in the course

Studies of adult education (see, for example, Tight, 1983 and Rogers, 1986) suggest that adult learners (and our mature students on counselling courses are always that) come with a very wide range of intentions, experience and learning abilities; that, in order to succeed, they need to share in the setting of goals; and that to optimize their learning they must be actively engaged in learning strategies, and not be passive recipients of someone else's wisdom or un-wisdom. A significant tension, however, and a source of considerable personal learning, is that adults new to or returning to study also bring often high anxiety and strong dependency needs. Grow's (1991) 'staged self-directed model', outlined earlier, gives some help with that tension: over time, adults can, and do, learn to learn differently, especially more autonomously.

There are many models of counselling training but some trends can be identified which have particular relevance for personal development. The general movement, in the thirty years existence of such training's existence in Britain, has been in the direction of *andragogy* rather than *pedagogy*. That is, people engage in a process that has shared goal setting, a valuing of existing experience, active rather than passive learning opportunities, an acceptance of maturity and developmental growth, recognition of a need to know and practical application of learning, all bearing out as Allman (1983) has stressed 'that a basic tenet of adult education (read counselling training) is to provide educational experiences that facilitate the development of control'. In particular, training has increasingly emphasized experiential learning (Rogers, 1983), learning with personal significance that is alive and useful; which moves in a feedback loop from concrete experience, to reflective observation to abstract conceptualizing and then to active experimentation, putting into practice what has been learned from the experience (Kolb, 1984).

The structures that deliver these learning models focus attention on and trigger much personal development; questions centre around the degree to which any course is staff or student-centred, structured or unstructured, tutor-led or self-directed. Depending on these decisions, different kinds of personal issues – or the same issues reached in different ways – will be stimulated in all members of a course community. Much personal exploration is triggered by experiences and questions around:

- How much support do I need?
- What helps me learn?
- How much help do I want to identify my own goals?
- What frustrates me in this learning situation?
- Do I feel cooperative or competitive with my fellow trainees?
- When do I feel most anxious?
- How much imposed structure do I need/enjoy/resent?
- What do I need from course leaders?

That last question raises, of course, the key issue of trainer/tutor/facilitator/leader style and its contribution, along with the structure of the course and the learning models available, to the climate of the learning group (see also Chapter 9). There are many models, such as the continuum from autocratic to laissez-faire to democratic, translated by Rogers (1986) into the lion-tamer, the entertainer and the cultivator. What is significant for counselling training is that each has a contribution for different purposes at different points and each will raise particular thoughts, feelings, anxieties or concerns in individual course members, thus triggering some of the incidental but core material for personal development work. A trainer colleague described herself as follows:

> *When I am the lion-tamer, I offer clarity and strength, I am a good container for the group and firm – in a helpful way – about, especially, the non-negotiable parts of the course; trainees often want to fight me on some issues, but I feel grounded and solid; often, the group process seems 'clean'. As entertainer, I can 'perform' and be challenging in quite an exciting way, be quite charismatic – the group can then feel rather unpredictable and scary for some members, though very alive for others. When I am the cultivator, I am most engaged and genuine, I think, and open to real debate with trainees: that's when they feel valued by me and the climate is at its most creative and warmest. I think people are more prepared to take risks then.*

The key implication for trainers is how to manage a range of structures, styles and focus and still communicate effectively and consistently the core qualities of empathy, acceptance and genuineness. These, it is generally agreed are at the heart of all helping relationships and will directly contribute to the climate of warmth, stimulus and safety in the course as a whole which I believe is essential for the most productive adult learning.

Balancing acts

There are a number of ways, in addition to the demands spelled out in the previous section, in which the struggle for balance will contribute to personal development work. There are, I know, people who despise a search for balance as insipid, lacking in excitement and somehow avoiding real challenge, yet I am sure that it is key in terms of providing the most fruitful environment for personal growth. Balance in this sense does not mean a lack of energy, passion or even extremes; it does mean allowing space, time, and attention for as many needs as possible to be met at different times. Some key aspects of balance include the provision in the group for individual needs to be met; for group needs to be addressed; and for essential tasks – for example, to work with integrity with clients! – to be achieved. Imbalance is inevitable at times, and will produce much to work on. There will be moments when the needs of trainees, triggered perhaps by outside events or crises in their own lives, will have to have attention and the group needs and tasks will be suspended for a time. In parallel, the balance of support and challenge – from trainers to trainees, trainees to trainers, course members to each other and each individual to herself or himself – has to be constantly sought, which again will be different for every individual at any stage in the course. When the balance is right, there is much personal learning (not least in the parallels with counselling) and when it is wrong, given adequate opportunities to explore responses and difficulties, much of value will be identified and available for exploration and possible resolution.

Again, balance can be considered in terms of expectations of commitment to the course, the place of the course in the broader life of trainers and trainees and the degree of self-sharing about each in and with the other. All these questions will inevitably be affected by any individual's values, history, theoretical orientation and readiness.

Critical incidents

A key way in which individual personal development is affected, fed or stimulated is the progress through the very history and time-frame of the course. This is itself, of course, a microcosm of the life span and life space issues discussed earlier. Everything which occurs, from someone expressing an interest in such training through to post-course experience with clients, has potential for self-exploration and personal learning. Some examples – and trainers will have their own specific versions – include

- the selection process;
- arrival on the course;
- first day, first few weeks;
- finding friends and noticing antipathies;
- performance anxiety at skills work, first assignment, first client;
- achievement/failure issues at any stage;
- individuals in crisis;
- assessment;
- self-disclosure;
- conflicts in the group;
- endings.

The ways in which the course as a whole, as well as individuals, manages these moments will affect the potential for and nature of the personal learning involved.

Modelling

Much is claimed for the crucial importance of modelling in counselling training: as the proverb says, 'I cannot hear what you say for the thunder of what you are!' In terms of personal development, this expectation, in particular, places great demands on trainers, the course they run, the climate they create, the ways in which they conduct their relationships with colleagues, their own lives, their ability to use self-disclosure appropriately, the ways they nurture themselves and maintain health and strength, and perhaps most of all, especially in training where the quality of the working relationship is paramount, their congruence and integrity. I feel exhausted just writing all that! It is important that trainers and the processes of the course itself, selection, assessment, feedback, evaluation and so on demonstrate the core commitment to openness, genuineness, honesty, and integrity. And yet, the reality that trainers are less than perfect, though struggling for integrity, may be at least as significant in prompting potential personal development for everyone. We are fallible, we are human; if a counselling course and all its members are unable to accept and demonstrate that, then there is something unhealthy at the heart of the learning process. If the key to quality training is self-challenge, linked with creative work with others, then there will be at least as much to learn from trainers and from a course, where people make mistakes, where the best intentions are sometimes distorted ... and where the culture is then to own difficulties, explore them, work for understanding and trust, remedial action if possible and acceptance if not. Where individuals hold on grimly to 'blame and shame' processes and feelings, then I have some serious concerns about the stage of their personal development – and that is so whether they are trainees or trainers.

Skills

The skills that are needed for personal development, for trainers and trainees, are very important, not least because they are also key skills in counselling. They involve being pro-active and pro-social; exploring oneself and being available to and for others. At the heart of the process are skills of questioning, reflecting, listening to oneself, immediacy, self-disclosure, values clarification, creativity, self-challenge, conflict resolution, being able to discriminate, make choices and accept the consequences, and, perhaps, most of all, making connections.

What I have written here should raise more questions than answers. All the elements in the preceding chapters – the possible curriculum for personal development, the trainees, the trainers and the nature of a course itself – provide the context for Chapters 7, 8 and 9: the methods and techniques, the micro-issues of actually stimulating, undertaking and managing personal development.

SOME QUESTIONS

1   How might trainers identify and explore their attitudes to the potential power and influence in their role?

2   Are trainers 'change-agents' in others' lives? Or is that question an example of grandiosity?

3   What are the gains and costs of co-tutoring? How might it challenge a trainer?

4   If trainers are key models, what should they model – or not model?

5   If you are a trainer or trainee, what kind of climate, in your view, optimizes learning and how can it be created?

SEVEN

How do we do it (I)?

Personal development through individual exploration

Counselling training, in most theoretical orientations, involves the whole person of the trainee; the theme of this and the next two chapters is that personal development should, in parallel, be in focus through all course activities.

Traditional course design tended to compartmentalize the learning in any course into theory, skills, work with clients and work on self, as if labelling a separate box would ensure that that part of the training took place. In terms of personal development, there are parallels with curriculum evolution in education, in areas such as health and careers education or equal opportunities and oppression. First, an argument that such learning will happen incidentally, almost by osmosis; this denies it status and legitimacy. Then, a recognition that such a discipline can and should exist as a separate focus in its own right; not until it does, will sufficient attention, rigour or depth be reached. Once a body of knowledge, experience and methodology has been identified in a discrete subject area, the curriculum thinking roller-coaster then decrees that it is so important that it must occur throughout all other areas of the curriculum, be integrated, linked and applied to and through everything else ... then it again runs the risk of losing status and disappearing. Some counselling courses have paid lip-service to the concept of work on self, but assumed that 'it' will somehow happen as if by magic, either through the trainees simply being there and experiencing all other aspects of the training or that studying theories about self and psychology will transmute magically into personal learning. Other courses, in contrast, place such an emphasis on self and the personal growth of the trainee that clients, ethics and the world of counselling seem relatively unimportant and all course activities seem geared to, at worst, egocentric, even self-indulgent exploration, which has little bearing on competence or application to counselling as an intentional activity. Yet others accept the need for balance of activities and focus, yet corral personal development either into trainees' personal counselling/therapy (see the next section of this chapter) or into the labelled box of personal development groups (see Chapter 9) or, at best, sometimes into both. If the person of the counsellor is of central significance in relation to the client, none of these positions will alone provide for sufficient work on self in counselling training. Personal development must have a discrete, separate identity, *and* be integrated in all other aspects of training; it must have a clear focus to legitimize it and recognize its centrality, yet it must also be drawn on to illuminate theory, skills and counselling practice and be extended and developed through those other activities. 'Inductive training', with its emphasis on exploring personal meaning in order to promote awareness, and 'deductive training', which prioritizes skills learning in order to increase counsellor proficiency, need personal development at the heart of their activities. Both approaches, which should not be seen as either/or, must consider how all the teaching and learning strategies of the course deepen self and other awareness, in order that trainees become more effective counsellors.

Underpinning all of this is the premise that counselling training is best delivered through *experiential* learning: 'a process which directly acknowledges, welcomes, values and uses the existing knowledge and competence of those being taught'. It is 'particularly appropriate where (what is in focus) are people's deeply held beliefs and attitudes or involves emotionally-charged or value-laden material' (Hobbs, 1992). Other significant elements include an emphasis on the skills of *reflecting on experience*, the importance of a *supportive climate* in which trust can develop and some sense of *integration and connection* amongst all the course elements, theories, skills, clients, supervision, personal history and present experience. Most important, perhaps, will be the ways in which any course manages the tension between the need for *safety* and known solid ground and the excitement of *risk* and change, together with the balance of support and challenge which makes that possible. With those in mind, this chapter and the next two will outline three principal approaches to personal development work: through trainees working as individuals in a range of reflective ways; through structured activities and exercises in all aspects of the course; and through work in groups.

PERSONAL DEVELOPMENT THROUGH INDIVIDUAL EXPLORATION

Learning to reflect is the key to increased self-awareness and personal development: on our experience in interactions with others, on the relationship between our own past and the present and on our unique patterns of reactions and responses. Kelly (1955), promoting personal construct theory, suggested, 'You are not the victim of your own autobiography, but you may become the victim of the way you interpret (it)'. Sartre (1934) emphasized, from the existential viewpoint, 'We are our choices, with the freedom to redesign our lives by those choices; and Rogers (1961) stressed the importance of the counsellor being able to retain her own identity while grasping the client's world. None of that is possible without the skills of reflection, insight and making connections: as the novelist EM Forster said, 'Only connect!' – a fine logo for counsellors in training!

These skills can be learned and increased through a range of activities which a trainee counsellor undertakes essentially on her own, not in direct relationship with other course members, though she may, of course, share her learning with others after the event, in a fruitful cycle of personal exploration (see Figure 7.1). She may be facilitated in some aspects of this individual work by another experienced worker, whether counsellor, supervisor, or trainer/tutor; this is different than reciprocal work with peers through structured activities.

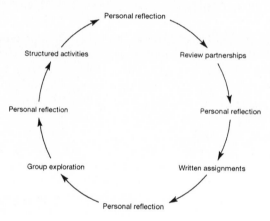

Figure 7.1 *Cycle of personal exploration*

These individual activities include a trainee's personal counselling, supervision, and tutorials; journal keeping – a record of her learning journey – and other creative methods of recording; reading creatively and responding to other forms of artistic/therapeutic stimulus.

Personal counselling

This represents one of the two extreme positions in traditional counselling training: that personal development 'happens' either in named groups set up for that purpose or in individual counselling/therapy. Some of the issues around personal counselling were outlined in Chapter 2: limited proven effectiveness of counselling for trainees; previous experience of counselling as a criterion for selection; questions of timing – when it might be most useful – and trainee readiness; attitudes towards it from different theoretical orientations; congruence, or not, between the model of counselling received and the core training model; whether it is more or less helpful if trainee and counsellor are the same gender, of similar age and ethnicity; and its significance as a chosen rather than imposed activity and as a safety net during counselling training.

Safety nets are indeed important, especially if they increase the possibility of risk taking, and release creative 'stretching' of the self, rather than inhibit experiments in doing or being. This is the strongest argument for trainees undertaking personal counselling while on a course: to extend the opportunities for focused reflection on thoughts, feelings, responses and behaviour triggered by the new or newly perceived experiences of becoming a counsellor. If counselling training is to be effective, then it should extend individual horizons, broaden understanding of others, increase acceptance of human variations – in short, expose trainees to much that is new. Inevitably, then, trainees may have triggered for them:

- unresolved personal issues (for example, family experiences and their relationship to being in groups; attitudes to authority or intimacy);
- sudden and unexpected questioning of beliefs and values previously taken for granted (such as, critical judgements of other people's religious frameworks which the trainee may now be learning to empathize with and accept);
- awareness of the implications of their own developmental stage or life space or transition and its discomforts (for example, for a middle-aged woman the new and exciting sense of identity and confidence which can grow while on a course can contrast sharply with a stable but now apparently boring and humdrum long marriage);
- and, perhaps most of all, the draining and stressful experiences of feeling inadequate, frightened, angry, bored, or any other 'unacceptable' feeling, in actual work with clients.

To have a safe space where any of these reactions can be explored seems vital; this should not, of course, be primarily in the service of personal growth, but in order to optimize learning from the course and enhance ability to work with clients. All of us who have trained as counsellors have experienced reactions to clients which we do not like or do not understand; have noticed blocks and resistances to emotional responses; and have needed help in bringing into awareness blind spots and distortions in our attitudes to others. Some of the work on these difficulties will be done through all the activities on the course; personal counselling with a focus only on the trainee can offer significantly intense time and attention to ensure that less is avoided and more awareness and self-knowledge results. The primary purpose, then, of personal counselling during training, is to enhance the trainee's competence and confidence in working with clients. These will again be reinforced if all aspects of the counselling experience are reflected on as part of the process:

- What is it like seeking a counsellor?
- What does someone need in order to discover what kind of counsellor he or she wants?
- How difficult is the first session?
- What helps or hinders the development of the relationship?
- How does it feel to be in the role of client?
- What is the experience of being a client with a counsellor of this orientation (ideally the same as the core training model)?
- What are the blocks to effective working?
- What is it like to pay for the service?

While the process of answering all these questions will extend a trainee's professional understanding, the content and issues of the counselling can only contribute to personal development, in increasing self- and other awareness, extending understanding of inner strengths and blocks and developing clarity of, purpose for and commitment to one's self as a person as well as a counsellor.

The timing and duration of personal counselling will vary according to a trainee's previous experience, state of readiness for training and ability to afford it: the last a very real consideration. The ideal model – certainly in terms of boundaries – would involve trainees working with paid professional counsellors entirely separate from the course. The reality is that trainees, already paying increasingly high fees, may have to settle for peer counselling with fellow trainees, or being 'practice clients' for members of other courses.

There are other issues, too, in addition to cost, such as availability of counsellors from a range of ethnic backgrounds, those with experience of disability or of differing sexual orientations, which limit access for many to counselling training. The BAC *Code of Ethics and Practice for Trainers* (revised 1995) stresses that the provision of counselling for trainees must be 'independent of the training context and any assessment procedures'; indeed, that 'The roles of trainee and client must be kept separate during the training; where painful personal issues are revealed, trainers are responsible for suggesting and encouraging further in-depth work outside the training context.' This is, of course, a 'boundary' issue which different counselling orientations will see in different ways (see the discussion on the facilitation of personal development groups in Chapter 9). In practice, the initial identification and response to such issues may well occur in one-to-one work with trainers/tutors (see section on tutorials below), since a trusting relationship will already be in place. However, a developmental counselling relationship may be most helpful and ethically appropriate for the trainee if it is with someone other than the trainer. Dryden and Feltham

(1994) suggest, in terms of timing, that personal counselling might be particularly helpful in the second year of a course, following experience in year one of personal development groups: this is a helpful, pragmatic suggestion, but it removes the possibility of the interactive process of taking learning from the one experience to the other. This can deepen and extend a trainee's understanding and insight, as, for example, she tries out in a group new behaviours identified in personal exploration. If personal counselling can co-exist with the group experience and with all the other structured, interactive activities of the course, there is perhaps the optimum possibility of fulfilling the BAC Course Recognition requirements for 'regular and systematic approaches to self-awareness work ... congruent with the course rationale'.

Supervision

This is the main vehicle for trainee professional development and for focusing on the needs of and work with clients. Increasingly, the models of supervision used for courses are developmental, relationship and process orientated rather than the more traditional task-based casework approach. The trainee will identify and note personal and emotional reactions to clients (such as strong attraction, unexplained hostility or a feeling of distrust), address them as appropriate in the supervision session, then highlight them for taking, if necessary, for further exploration to personal counselling, exploration in groups or other reflective situations. Inevitably, these two activities – supervision and personal counselling – run in tandem; I have little patience with the arbitrary (and unworkable) division which some practitioners try to erect – that supervision is the place *only* for clients' issues. It is inescapable, firstly, that the person of the counsellor is present in the relationship with the client and, secondly, that sometimes personal issues for the counsellor have to be addressed in supervision in order to clear sufficient emotional and cognitive space to work usefully on the counselling process and the needs of the client. Balance and focus, as ever, are perhaps what are at issue: in a trainee's personal counselling, her feelings and issues will be in the forefront, though clients and what they trigger will be present too; in supervision, clients and their concerns and ethical needs must be in the forefront, but the trainee, her responses and needs are inevitably – and properly – present, if usually in the background. Supervision is certainly one of the places, during and after training, where a trainee's personal development must be put clearly in context as in the service of the clients. Yet, central personal issues of growth may be highlighted which are formative, and so still developing (a counsellor working with bereaved clients may 'discover' unfinished grieving for her own parents, triggered by, for example, a need to limit the expression of distress by a client) or normative, clarifying appropriate standards for a counsellor (the desire, for instance, to allow a particular counselling relationship to become a friendship).

Tutorials

This is a third arena for individual exploration facilitated by skilled support, this time from an experienced trainer/tutor. Perhaps because the concept of tutorials – a one-to-one or one-staff-to-two trainees exchange – is rooted in higher education, it is less frequently seen as a key element in promoting personal development in counselling training. It must also be recognized that such intensive staff support is an expensive resource which cannot be afforded in all training contexts. Where it is possible, I am very clear from my own experiences over the years as a student and a trainer and especially from feedback from trainees who have worked with me and other colleagues, that a well-conducted tutorial provides one of the most fertile opportunities for personal development. The essence of a tutorial is:

- to give an individual trainee time, space and attention;
- to reflect on the learning in process;
- to explore specifically the training relationship between trainee and peers, trainees and trainers;
- to facilitate the making of connections between cognitive and affective responses;
- to link insights from professional experiences (work with clients, supervision and skills practice), with growing personal awareness (through reflection, for example, in personal counselling, reading and writing);
- and, above all, having clarified and deepened these understandings, to set new goals and objectives through prioritizing tasks and needs, for the next stage of learning and growth.

The tutorial relationship is not a counselling relationship: it has much more of a dual focus, the learner/trainee herself, of course, but also the tasks and processes of learning. An effective tutor will use counselling skills to build a 'working alliance' and to offer a balance of support and challenge, but should also model cognitive skills, demonstrate expertise where appropriate, enable the trainee to face and explore learning blocks and use the acquisition of study skills as a vehicle for making sound and subtle connections across all the areas of study in counselling training – work with clients, theory, skills learning, supervision, reading for purpose, writing assignments and working on self. The tutorial also provides the chance to begin clarifying concerns to be taken to personal counselling. The ability to analyse (break down) and synthesize (build up) ideas and issues also involves skills which, I believe, are transferable to counselling, since a counsellor needs to use both head and heart – which a successful tutorial demonstrates. I have often been very moved when a trainee, working at considerable depth, successfully confronts learning or training relationship difficulties or makes connections of significance, which affect self-perception or ways of relating to others in the training process. I recall a woman who was a twin and had always seen herself as 'the stupid twin' – since the other one had all the shared brain!; her sense of achievement and joy when she discovered she could write excellent academic assignments had us both in tears.

Good quality tutorials can offer to both parties the sense of a truly connected working partnership and of being part of exciting personal movement and growth. There are some dangers of paternalistic inequality if the tutor/trainer becomes too hooked by the expert role which can be engaged; yet to share expertise and facilitate another person's ability to learn and move is for me as a trainer one of the most satisfying of training processes. Working with mature adults, too, with the panorama of life experiences and developmental or crisis issues they bring with them, is a humbling experience, a constant reminder of the *effort* involved in learning and personal development. Many trainees have to overcome great obstacles, and yet demonstrate – given opportunity, resources and adequate support – considerable courage and potential. Tutorials provide a key forum for personal development and a central place for tutors in any course to communicate respect and valuing to individual trainees. They also offer opportunities for trainers to make visible their judgements through feedback to trainees, which may form part of any assessment procedures.

Journal-keeping

It is said that, before beginning every period of prayer, Saint Ignatious Loyola asked himself, 'What do I truly want?' That might indeed be a useful question for any trainee beginning to use a journal as part of her learning process. One of the central aims of counselling training is to produce reflective practitioners who are able to develop their own 'internal supervisor', extend and maintain awareness of self and others and continue to integrate all aspects of their learning from the course and outside it. Many training courses have introduced learning journals to promote these aims, paralleling the interest in diaries, personal recording and self exploration in other twentieth century (and earlier) movements such as personal growth, women's studies and life history exploration. Essentially, a learning journal provides a forum for 'creative introspection', the reflective central element in the learning cycle. This enables an individual to reflect purposefully on experience, making personal meaning after action of any kind and before planning or implementing any further action. Diaries and journals of this kind have little to do with 'outdated notions and misconceptions of ... self-discipline, a dutiful record of events, a narcissistic self-absorption, an escape from reality, or a nostalgic adherence to the past' (Rainer, 1980), but are rather a 'practical psychological tool ... to express feelings without inhibition, recognize and alter self-defeating habits of mind, and come to know and accept that self which is you ... It can help you understand your past, discover joy in the present and create your own future'. Rainer stressed the potential of journals for tapping 'valuable inner resources' and named Jung, Milner, Progoff and Nin as key models, who recognized 'a need in the modern world to reflect calmly upon knowledge that comes from within'. Milner (1934), for example, publishing under the pen-name, Joanna Field, used her journal as a practical tool for living, identifying feelings and needs and planning action, as well as a means of self-insight. Progoff (1975), using a systematic, structured approach called an 'Intensive Journal', described the process as a 'continuing confrontation of oneself in the midst of life', a way of exploring one's life from many perspectives, finding the connecting threads, linking past and present and making meaning through reflection.

In counselling training, more specifically, keeping and using such a journal is a way of optimizing learning: increasing awareness, making connections and integrating reflective work on self with understanding of theory, practical skills, work with clients and insights from personal counselling and supervision. It should be a live 'work in progress' record of the trainee's developing self-as-counsellor, noticing and exploring the individual's experience of and interaction with the course, other group members, the trainers, the world and process of counselling, the interplay of personal past and present and of the course with the rest of life. The aims and purposes of a learning journal include:

- reflecting on experience, thoughts, feelings and behaviours
- exploring ideas, reactions, changes in self and others
- clarifying personal beliefs, attitudes, values
- evaluating movement in understanding, skills, knowledge
- setting objectives for the next stage of learning and growth
- monitoring assumptions, achievement and blocks.

In particular, themes which might come into focus are:

- relationships (with peers, staff, clients, colleagues, self and 'significant others');
- ways of being (in all aspects of the course – and what helps, hinders, blocks, frightens, motivates, challenges and supports);
- levels of participation (what turns you on or off);
- issues (what comes into the foreground, what is in the background; what connects with or triggers past patterns of response or emotion; what systems' influences affect you);
- what personal learning is there for the trainee as counsellor (strengths? limits? what do you seek out? what do you avoid? what do you need in any situation?); and, finally,
- what future development do you need to plan for (direction? goals? personal agenda? handicaps?).

Creative journal keeping fosters, above all, the ability to take responsibility for our own learning, prompts the (central) search for personal meaning and involves a more intense relationship with ourselves, a need to listen to our experience in an intimate and open way. The outcomes should be exploratory and questioning, open and uncensored, not labelling and closed. Any learning journal entry is likely to contain lots of question marks, since noting unanswered questions is a key part of personal and professional development; those issues may hold the seeds of the next stage of learning and seeking. A journal extract from a trainee six weeks into his course read as follows:

> *Buzz from skills work still there today – feels like skiing (?) when I get it right – what will it be like when I feel in difficulties? Felt much more comfortable with Mary than with Jack when giving feedback. Do I expect him to laugh at me? Who does he remind me of? Still very tense in the large group – ? like school? competitive? What if I try to speak earlier in the session next week?*

Some trainees find the process of keeping a journal a burden, while others are enabled to release great creativity. At its best, the process can provide a vehicle for linking left-brain (rational, cognitive) activity and right-brain (creative, intuitive) energy. Any stimulus and any recording method can be valuable: continuous, formally-structured prose is not the only, or indeed perhaps the most valuable, way of capturing the rich and dense experience of immersion in counselling training. Giving time and attention to reflecting on any session of a course is the starting point for allowing relaxation, visualization, images, and so on, to bring into focus any material worth capturing – and that means *any* material which is spontaneous rather than rehearsed, reflective rather than merely descriptive, and alive rather than dead. Form and structure can be entirely individual; content and process will be different for everyone; and the detailed media of expression can include poetry, prose, drawing, doodles, cartoons, colours, lists, metaphors, similes, fairy stories, photomontages, literature quotations, or, indeed, tape recordings, musical extracts or any other means of capturing the essence, meaning and value of any aspect of the training experience in a way that allows for exploration and further learning. The individual's task is to 'find her voice', in order to articulate in a creative and stimulating manner, as she becomes a counsellor, her personal journey of awareness and insight.

There are many journal techniques, such as writing a self-description in the third person, which allows some distancing of perception; drawing 'maps of consciousness' or free-intuitive drawing to capture unconscious images; making lists of feelings, thoughts or fears triggered by an experience in the course; writing or drawing a dialogue with yourself or another person to unpick or clarify some unresolved issue. (For more detail, see

Rainer, 1980; Progoff, 1975 and (Milner, Field, 1934). An inexperienced counsellor beginning a course described herself in the third person as follows:

> *Joan is showing the group her social self at present; she is quite good at small talk in the coffee breaks, she seems fairly confident, has taken trouble to dress casually, she is working quite hard to blend into the group. Underneath she is feeling very scared and rather small; if anyone scratched the surface, she feels she might cry very easily.*

All of these techniques can be used and adapted for counselling training purposes. There are, however, some key issues for debate. Unless the learning journal is truly integrated into the learning cycle of all course activities, some trainees find it hard to motivate themselves to sustain consistent and regular recording – the task becomes an effort rather than a creative support. Some people genuinely feel at a loss in creative terms and have no experience of articulating their thoughts, feelings and difficulties; they need lots of help and preparation in order to gain confidence to begin and risk. There are questions about how such material is monitored and by whom, if it is assessed and how. Some courses insist on trainers seeing journal material on a regular basis, to ensure its existence and quality. My own view is that the original material produced by trainees should be respected as formative and private, while it is reasonable for trainers to expect to see regularly, perhaps once or twice a year, a summative report, profile or statement of learning, in order that trainees can demonstrate their capacity for reflection, increasing insight, recognition of strengths and blocks and, most of all, some sense of growth and movement. This process can be helped by, firstly, having trainees negotiate a 'personal learning contract', which is then at the heart of the learning journal and to which they feel some commitment; and, secondly, building into the course structure some reinforcing patterns, such as 'review partners' or small 'journal groups' who meet regularly to help each other articulate and deepen the learning from their journal explorations. Regular response to key questions can also be useful, such as:

- What have I learned today?
- What helped me learn?
- What got in the way?
- Who did I feel close to/distant from?
- What discomforts did I feel?
- What image/colour/symbol captures the essence of that session?

Used in this way, the learning journal can be the fulcrum of all the personal development activities on the course, the place where reflective awareness can increase the value of all personal exploration and ensure the existence of a purposeful and concrete learning cycle linked directly with the trainee's progress as counsellor and always-developing mature adult. The full potential of journal work is rarely achieved in training courses, although much attention is, in theory, paid to it. As I write this, the image of 'map-making' occurs to me as both a metaphor and an acronym for the significance of learning journal work. The metaphor seems apt: maps involve routes and connections to and between significant points; crossroads and choices of direction; signposts, which may be vital in reaching some kind of journey's end; distinctive 'markers' on the way – of places, people, history and geography; indications of safe, clear routes and those with hazards or 'road works' ahead; and, although some features of the landscape may be relatively fixed, much can change over time, so that any map is relevant for only a limited period, must be constantly updated and superseded by successive editions. Maps, too, can exist in a very wide range of detail and depth and for different purposes and can be accessible in different degrees to other people, given an adequate key to the symbols! All these features are true of learning journals, summarized in the acronym: MAPMAKING:

Motivation	Assistance	Preparation	Monitoring
Awareness	Knowledge	Insight	Nurturing
Growth.			

Journals are essentially the record of personal learning, selectively shared and deepened through summative extracts, explored further in tutorials or with peers, but clearly the property of the individual. The potential value of the concepts, insights and transferable learning for others in the group is often wasted, unless some way of sharing appropriately is devised. Summative accounts or personal profiles, of course, can be exchanged in peer support groups or partnerships, both for feedback and for facilitating self and others' learning. An interesting model (Berman, 1994) is one in which selected extracts of journals in progress are anonymously read or shared on paper amongst the whole group, so that particularly significant learning issues or difficulties can be captured, conceptualized and clarified. The degree to which learning journals are central or peripheral to the course learning cycle will vary enormously from course to course; if personal development is seen as central to all activities, a journal will be a key way of harnessing and processing all elements of that learning. A journal can have different significance for each individual at different times: it can be a safety-valve, a crucial mechanism for making learning concrete and specific, a 'transitional object' security blanket to which deepest thoughts, feelings and fears can be safely expressed, the place for reality testing, or an arena, reinforced by exploration with others, for establishing identity, accepting and having dialogue amongst sub-personalities and setting objectives for self-as-counsellor growth.

Other writing and recording

Miller Mair (Mair, 1989) explored the importance of 'personal knowing …
in the midst of knowing what we dare to know, being shaped towards blind-
ness by what we fear to see'. He advocates searching for the precision and
subjectivity of expression which poetry, for example, can offer and quotes
TS Eliot: 'at the moment when one writes, one is what one is … '. Writing
creatively in poetry or prose and risking the expression of intuition, half-
knowing, or sensing, might add much to our understanding, especially if we
can give ourselves permission to be tentative, to play with language and
metaphor rather than depend on factual, prescriptive communication. Mair
suggests that 'We tend to banish what is tentative and growing in favour of
what is solid and simply seen'; he advocates 'a widening of attention … so
that we sense more of what we already do'. Embedded in this proposal is an
acceptance that our subjective selves are significant, that scientific language
and objective facts can take us only a limited way in opening the mysteries
of being human. Mair argues that 'Our places of human habitation are
mostly invisible. We will have to conjure out of invisibility the worlds that
we inhabit. To do this we need a poetic imagination to speak of our experiencing … '. So, to write poetry, to describe our feelings, sensations and
doubts through stories and metaphor, to reflect on our responses by drawing, painting, using colour to seek meaning, or by sculpting our life space at
any moment using natural materials – all these are methods of deepening
insight, struggling for communication of our place in whatever story (or
stories) we find ourselves.

I can identify strongly with Mair's statement that 'We know more than
we can say and have to learn sometimes to say what we do not know'. I also
know how risky it feels to embark on journeys when I feel unsure of the language or customs of the country – yet how much I learn and experience
when I do! Some trainees – and trainers – have little confidence in writing
creatively, using drawing, visual or physical media with which to communicate; when they (and I) do risk new forms of 'journeying', the power and
potential for both clearer awareness and vivid communication can be very
moving. I learned a good deal recently in trying to write down my own sensations and process in a week when I constantly felt myself to be a charac-
ter in the wrong story: feeling like Eeyore lost in *Wind in the Willows*,
instead of at home in *The House at Pooh Corner*! The following extract from
a trainee's poem suggests the power of her feelings at a point of struggle
half-way through her course:

The wind of failure buffets me; I cannot stand.
I find no place to hide and have no
Sense of strengthened self to shield me from the storm of others' fear.
The child inside is crying in the dark …

Encouraging trainees (and trainers!) to write, draw, shape and generally express themselves and their reflective exploration creatively can be a powerful catalyst for personal development; it is also a significant way of demonstrating some of the central values of counselling: autonomy, individuality and respect for individual differences. If counsellors-in-training are enabled to value and release their own creativity with its potential for insight and growth, they may also be able to transmit something of the same stimulus to their clients. As with all methods of individual exploration, the most fruitful work may occur when sharing what has been produced with others, in pairs or small groups, in tutorials or counselling, so that further reflection can deepen understanding and personal meaning. We must, though, also recognize that such a sharing and outwardly reflective process is not always appropriate or helpful; the value of creative expression is sometimes embedded in the experience of the moment and may be diluted or distorted if too much articulation is automatically expected, in a formulaic way. Time and distance may be needed before the particular value of any experience or expression becomes clear: Wordsworth's 'recollection in tranquillity' expresses the potential value of reflection in an unforced way over time, in order that learning and understanding can emerge.

Similarly, although some trainers might see the products of such creative reflection as all belonging in a learning journal, I have separated them out in a way which might feel safer and be freeing for some trainees. Others, of course, will comfortably include every aspect of their personal exploration and creativity in a journal which they make available to all. While confidentiality receives endless attention on counselling courses, the issue of privacy, the degree to which trainees must expect to 'bare all' symbolically to others, is rarely discussed. As an adult educator, I believe that learning articulated to others is more likely to be useful, yet respect for individual autonomy is a central value in counselling. Balancing this view – the right to keep self-knowledge private, especially if it also involves other people – with the expectation of openness and self-disclosure is sometimes a tension in counselling training.

Reading

Finally, in this section on personal development through individual exploration, I arrive, in a sense, where I began on my own journey of counsellor self-awareness and growth, in the most private of learning activities: reading. Imaginative engagement with literature of all kinds can directly and indirectly contribute to individual understanding of self, others and human experience. I remember reading, when I was about ten years old, a children's adventure story in which someone nearly drowned in quicksand – the vivid description is with me still, together with the sense of tension and the smell of fear. I recall, too, as a student reading for an English degree, the power and thrill of making contact with characters in great novels and plays: beginning to understand the terrible struggle in a variety of human lives between convention and desire, for instance, in the novels of Thomas Hardy or in the Jacobean tragedies. Those glimpses into the felt experience of other lives and times is one of the contributions which literature can offer, so extending our working knowledge of human life. Other art forms, such as painting, sculpture, images of all kinds can provide us with similar insights, if we are able to access them. One of the core aspects of personal development is, perhaps, learning to 'read' all sources of information about the human condition, though we may each, naturally, have our preferred medium. Literature is mine! We can learn more of the detail and fact about ages, stages, classes, cultures and ethos of lives very different than our own, which may help us be well-informed and educated, not easily surprised and ready for meeting in clients the astonishing range of ways of being human. To this end, it is relatively easy to list novels, plays and poems about grow-ing-up, such as Alice Walker's *The Color Purple* or Jeannette Winterson's *Oranges are Not the Only Fruit*; about bereavement and loss, from Audre Lord's *Cancer Journals*, to Jon Silkin's *Death of a Son*; or on relationships, for instance, D.H. Lawrence's *Sons and Lovers*, Alison Lurie's *Love and Friendship* or Arthur Miller's *Death of a Salesman*.

It is sometimes argued that reading is at best only a vicarious entry into others' lives and as such can add little to empathic understanding or self-knowledge. This is not my experience: richly written prose or poetry can stimulate cognitive and affective responses, extend imaginative understand-ing of people, other times or feelings, and increase flexibility and receptiv-ity to whatever is presented by clients or colleagues. In terms of personal development, reading can offer points of comparison and contrast which trigger fruitful exploration; our own empathic responses to the glimpses lit-erature provides of other people's lives can trigger rewarding questioning of patterns of reaction and understanding; and an increase in self- and other-awareness may be a valuable product of exposure to vividly written fiction, biography or history. I recall a trainee in his fifties saying how much he was learning about himself and his difficulties around intimacy from reading some of the poetry of Sylvia Plath, while another woman of thirty-five began to understand more of her anxiety about ageing and achievement after immersing herself in biographies of twentieth century politicians!

The potential value of literature for personal development can be further extended if we focus on our understanding of the symbolic meanings of language. Ben Knights (1995), in his aptly-entitled *The Listening Reader*, argues persuasively that reading is a form of experience which, through the interaction of the reader's presence with the literature, extends the reader as a person. The dialogue which takes place between the reader and the lan-guage of texts provides 'equipment for living', the development of empathic knowledge, imagination and language itself, in which to tell human experience. He suggests that literature offers the opportunity not only to learn more about human life and experience, but provides 'a laboratory of meaning in process': words are not absolute or unambiguous, they are part of people's 'struggle to make sense of their relations to others and to themselves'. At the heart of this view of the importance of language and literature – and central in my understanding of personal development – is the idea that 'human identity is not an essence, but is continually made and remade through language ... ': we make our own meanings of ourselves and our lives and are aware of ourselves as we do so.

Knights stresses that opening ourselves to literature and extending our ability to use and engage with language can increase our inner resources; that familiarity with stories, scripts and characters enables us to draw upon a 'full and abundantly populated inner world' in which, quoting Bruner (1986), 'stories ... provide ... a map of possible roles and possible worlds in which action, thought and self-definition are permissible (or desirable)'. If we have a wide enough repertoire and flexibility of language, we can, for ourselves and our clients, use it to frame new awarenesses, name the changes we might desire in our lives, and 'make meaning' of human experience. The ability to 'name' experiences and feelings can give us, perhaps, some power over them; making contact with universal myths and concepts can extend our range of possible worlds. The potential for literature to stimulate unexpected images and 'provoke us ... to draw on depths we have learned not to know we had' (Knights, 1995) offers us an almost unlimited resource for personal development. A particularly rich and dense source of fascinating 'prompts' for self-exploration, regardless of theoretical orientation, is *Shakespeare as Prompter* (Cox and Theilgaard, 1994). As the editors emphasize, Shakespeare 'furnishes examples of virtually every kind of human interaction. He also offers numerous illustrations of the subtle variations of the reflective self. Finally, he provides a variety of instances in which the nature of human identity is the central issue.' What more could be hoped for as an aid to personal development!

Reading, in a different way from listening and counselling, is an interpersonal and transactional activity. I am aware that the ability to read does not come easily to all, for physical, perceptual or other reasons, and that the intense pleasure and potential it has always had for me may be experienced as anxiety, inadequacy or frustration by others. Language deficiency, then, may limit personal development, but so may a lack of visual awareness and kinaesthetic or tactile abilities. All of us, trainees and trainers, should perhaps consider the opportunities we miss for extending our imaginative and cognitive potential by being open to all forms of creative communication.

All the above – counselling, supervision, tutorials, learning journals, writing/recording and reading – are ways in which trainee counsellors (and, of course, experienced counsellors, supervisors and trainers too!) can extend their own personal development through individual exploration. The next chapter will consider some of the interactive activities which can contribute to the same end.

SOME QUESTIONS

1 What reasons would you offer for or against personal counselling being essential for trainees?

2 Do you agree with the BAC view that counselling for trainees should be entirely separated from the 'training context and any assessment procedures'?

3 How would you differentiate between the kinds of learning available in supervision, counselling and tutorials?

4 Should learning journals be assessed?

5 What is your preferred medium for extending your understanding of the world?

EIGHT

How do we do it (II)?

Personal development through structured activities

There is a place for lectures in counselling training, since certain kinds of information can be most efficiently delivered to large groups in that didactic form. Most learning in the counselling field, however, needs to be connected with practice and with self, processed through real examples and is only useful if made concrete, specific and applied by the trainee in some way. Then, with Marshall McLuhan, we have to accept that 'the medium is the message' (quoted in Dainow and Bailey, 1988) and make learning opportunities active rather than passive, collaborative rather than expert-dominated, and personal rather than generalized. Most counselling training of any quality has moved in recent years towards such an active, particatory, experiential learning model, in keeping with some of the key principles of adult education already outlined. Significant in this approach is the reliance on structured activities in pairs, threes or fours (or any other appropriate subgroup number) to focus trainees' thinking or feeling, to process new ideas or techniques or to extend, apply and personalize theoretical concepts. All of these functions are important; and all can be paired explicitly or implicitly with promoting self-awareness and so contributing to personal development.

VALUE OF STRUCTURED ACTIVITIES

It is impossible to be specific about the use of structured exercises in every kind of training course: theoretical orientation, nature of the context, trainer style and skill will make every course different and the degree of such practice variable. I shall inevitably make generalizations which will have to be filled out or challenged by trainers of different persuasions. Whatever the differences, the gains of using such activities as the core of counselling training are many: different kinds of energies can be generated – interactive, fun, creative, physical energy; everyone in the group is involved – even to opt out demands some self-sharing and openness; dependency on the leader/trainer is reduced – there is an immediate sharing of responsibility; and minor and major change-processes can be triggered by the concrete experience of interpersonal exchange in a shared task, a pair listening exercise or counselling session, a role play, a simulation, a game or a creative activity of some kind. Again, any exchange with one or more group members will raise similarities and contrasts between people and with counselling interactions; may begin the identification of counter-transference issues, raw spots, blind spots, panic-buttons, unresolved sensitivities (chose the terminology depending on your orientation!); or will bring into focus resistance, reluctance or oppositional feelings which may well be very significant in the individual's development as a counsellor. Working intensively in pairs or with small numbers of peers offers intimacy, a greater feeling of safety and less threat, especially early in a course, than contributing in a large group.

Most of all, the gains of structured, interactive activities lie in the contribution to the 'climate' of any course. This is absolutely key in the success or failure of training, the promotion of trust, the opportunities for communicating and extending empathy, acceptance and genuineness and the possibility of a mutuality of involvement of all members of the course community. That, of course, is one of my core training values: I am aware it may not be shared by all readers, who may have very different training philosophies. To some trainers it may sound over-optimistic, even Pollyanna-ish. I recognize – and know from experience – that achieving those gains is not necessarily a smooth or painless process. Engaging in direct interaction and intimate exchange with peers, even if the eventual outcomes are trust, awareness and growth, may – indeed must – involve challenge, possibly conflict, uncomfortable feedback, at times distorted projections and, at worst, undermining negative attack.

PURPOSES, TIMING AND DEBRIEFING OF EXERCISES

The potential for personal development in such structured activities is in the way, in particular, they are debriefed and explored. The essential trainer skills lie less in setting up activities (though that is a fine and skilful art) but in ways of identifying and using the potential learning which stems from them. Effective counsellor trainers have in large measure the ability to structure opportunities and mechanisms for such debriefing and the sensitivity to maintain a receptive, safe-enough climate, with an appropriate balance (different at different times) of support and challenge. There are, in contrast, a worrying number of trainers who see exercises and activities as ends in themselves, with little awareness of the complexities, ethical issues and needs for trainee protection. There are often unintended consequences of a 'gung-ho' catapulting of relatively naive groups into powerful, potentially catalytic or cathartic activities: they may seem simple and innocuous but have the capacity to trigger subterranean rumblings of emotional, cognitive or physical dissonance and stress. It is impossible for trainers to predict every possible nuance of response in each individual; they do, however, have a responsibility to try to anticipate the process outcomes of any exercise or stimulus and be prepared to debrief and explore those outcomes with appropriate sensitivity and care.

Interactive structures can be in a variety of combinations of pair work, trios and fours (or other), all with different potential for personal learning: for example, an exchange amongst three people has less intensity and perhaps feels less pressured than a one-to-one confrontation, but it is possible for one member to feel excluded. Pair work allows for greater intimacy and also for direct challenge; activities in fours provide experience of intellectual debate and shared/contrasting views; while trios offer the chance of clarifying constructs: in what way are two of us alike and one of us different? Some structured activities can involve the whole large group, for example, when giving some specific feedback to each other (such as: How you have helped/hindered my learning this year) by lining up opposite each other in two lines, which move clockwise in a kind of loop, until each person has spoken with everyone else. Another example is when all members of a group observe the same activity (such as a supervision session) and then contribute to subsequent discussion from the point of view of a significant person, for example the (absent) client, the counsellor's work colleague, a member of the supervisor's peer support group and so on. It is important for trainers to work out the particular power of different combinations of numbers of trainees and relate those possibilities to the range of different purposes of any exercise.

Structured exercises can occur in any part of a course but there are certain points and purposes which are most likely to provide the opportunity for the dual functions of undertaking specific tasks plus intensifying personal awareness. These include the climate-setting, ice-breaking activities at the very start of any course; points in the life/time-line of a course – the beginning, any crisis point, first assignment, first video work, points of conflict, the ending; skills-learning including audiovisual work; processing theory and making links with practice; feedback-giving, especially in trios of, for example, client, counsellor and observer; support and challenge activities, such as regular support partnerships; and all activities promoting the reviewing and evaluating of individuals or the course as a whole. Potential outcomes will be affected by many factors, not least the timing of activities and their fit in overall course design and appropriateness in the moment. Trainers need both the ability to plan structured sessions in detail and the resources to change and adapt those plans, with a variety of contingency materials at hand, if the needs of the group prove a mismatch.

KINDS OF STRUCTURED ACTIVITIES

The five most powerful structured methods of promoting self-awareness and personal development are:

- Pair exercises centred on skills development in which both content and process are made available for reflection. These reflections are articulated and further explored after the event. An example would be spending ten minutes each way in twos, the listener practising active listening and avoiding interrogatory questions, while the speaker explores a choice she is facing in her life at present.
- Activities in threes: for example, short counselling sessions where each person takes a turn in the counsellor, client and observer role. These provide much material for all the participants about habitual ways of perceiving and patterns of responding, and offer essential practice in giving and receiving feedback, a key contribution to personal and professional development.
- The use of audio- and videotapes, particularly combined with the techniques of Interpersonal Process Recall (IPR) (Kagan, 1967). The latter involves someone reviewing a video or audio recording of her own interpersonal exchange (a counselling session, teaching group or management interview) immediately after the event, stopping the tape whenever she remembers anything, any awareness in the moment, emotional, cognitive, sensory or bodily, and deepening her understanding of the process with the help of another person called an 'enquirer'. Much audiovisual work in counselling training is aimed at skill development; IPR emphasizes in particular the growth of awareness, reinforced by the enquirer's encouragement to articulate and explore whatever is noticed. It is built on the premise that we notice but tune out a great deal more information, both internal and external, than we ever use in our interpersonal interactions. IPR does seem very effective in increasing awareness and developing the capacity for self-monitoring. Examples of enquirer questions, after the counsellor has stopped the tape with her initial observations are: Were you aware of any other feelings? Do you recall any image you had at that moment? Was there any tension anywhere in your body? Were there any thoughts which came with that?
- Further valuable structured mechanisms include any kind of role play or simulation activities, much values-clarification work and exploration of personal constructs, through exercises or briefings prepared beforehand by the trainer.
- Activities involving creative work – drawing, movement, collage, sounds – undertaken together then reflected on and explored in the pair or trio and then, perhaps, shared in the larger group.

The nature of the activities can involve verbal exchanges and listening exercises; using drawing or other artistic/creative media; prompting imagery, metaphors, similes, visualizations; designing and completing instruments, such as checklists or self-descriptions; encouraging brainstorming and recording on flipchart papers; or having non-verbal exchanges to illuminate communication or attitudinal issues and perceptions. Each of those modes will produce a variety of emotional and cognitive responses in any group of individuals. Sensitivity to those responses, providing opportunities for someone, for example, to disclose his or her anxieties and tension in non-verbal exchanges, are key skills for the trainer and will govern the nature of the learning environment she creates and sustains.

All these activities have potential for personal development; the keys to unlock it are, firstly, the climate in which people feel willing to risk themselves and, secondly, the nature, extent and sensitivity of discussion and debriefing after the activity. These must be facilitated and modelled at first by trainers; the core skills, however, can be actively promoted and developed throughout all course activities, so that trainees can support and help each other with the same processes. In addition, using personal material rather than role play in all of those activities offers many opportunities for self-exploration, increasing self-awareness and extending trainees' experiences of struggling towards congruence.

LEVELS OF EXPLORATION

There are at least four levels in which material from exercises can be explored, once awareness is stimulated and people gain practice in noticing, identifying, articulating and reflecting on what begins to emerge. That concept of *practice* is important: most of us in this culture are not experienced in such self-reflective processes and need to *learn* what might be available and how to access it. The levels are illustrated below by a simple exercise which might take place at the beginning of a course.

Share for ten minutes each in pairs the high and low spots of your educational experiences to date; listener to practise active listening skills. Possible reflections:

- *feelings* about the activity or the other person/s engaged in it and the insights and personal issues those feelings trigger. (The course member might find the low spots easy to identify – never felt confident about his own ability, bad experience with a teacher; strong anxiety and desire to censor a particular failure – overwhelming feelings that partner is much more successful, plus a powerful feeling of embarrassment – 'no right to be on the course'.)

- *thoughts and ideas* about the processes involved, evaluations of the content and process of any activity and connections between and across activities, personal concerns and counselling application and relevance. (Understanding of the power of comparison processes; self-fulfilling prophecy theories; awareness of reactions to what seemed like a judgemental response of partner. Need to check out perhaps misplaced comparisons and perceptions. Noticing own tendency to present as loser–win/lose construct.)
- *implications and application* to contexts outside the course, personal life, organizational/occupational relevance or broader cultural/social connections. (Relevance for dissatisfaction with present manager role in job – lacking confidence, non-assertive. Exploration of class issues in British culture – assumptions of inferiority. The effect on clients?)
- later *reflections in tranquillity*, personal reverberations over time, which may allow deeper or wider relevance and meanings to surface. (Sudden deep sadness a few days later about death of grandmother when trainee was thirteen; she had always been very validating – most positive influence in childhood.)

As that example suggests, there are, in any course, particular times and purposes for structured exercises which also contribute substantially to personal development.

EXAMPLES OF MULTI-PURPOSE ACTIVITIES

Many exercises involve active listening or skills practice. There are many others which have become well-known triggers in counselling training, the origins of which have been lost in the mists of training practice. Techniques from various counselling models such as gestalt, transactional analysis and psychosynthesis have also been used, adapted and absorbed into different approaches. As trainers, we should acknowledge gratefully those originators! (See Dainow and Bailey (1988) and Inskipp (1993 and 1996) for suggestions for structured activities.) Some examples follow of exercises which either explicitly or incidentally provoke awareness and personal development (the examples are illustrative only of many others). They can be used as the basis for listening skills practice in pair work, for practising self-disclosure and immediacy in twos, threes or fours, or for any other purpose in processing lecture material, experiences with clients, or other aspects of counselling theory and practice.

1. The so-called *Johari window* (developed, so it is said, by two people called Jo Luft and Harry Ingram). This is a very powerful framework, which can be used as an exercise specifically to promote self-awareness, and

returned to again and again at different levels and times in the course, in a spiral curriculum way, deepening understanding each time. Used with a partner, or in small groups, it provides the basis for opportunities to practise self-disclosure and so increase our ability to share our 'public self'; while asking for feedback from others can decrease our 'blind area' and help us towards more self-acceptance. A trainee recently found it very productive to explore what he had seen (and valued) as his style of trenchant intellectual questioning. Through feedback using the Johari window, he began to learn that fellow students saw him at times as pedantically 'nit-picking', while some clients felt intimidated by the sharp edge and voice he sometimes inadvertently carried over to counselling. Acknowledging that we all have an unknown part of ourselves and that, as counsellors, we have a duty to decrease that as much as possible, also involves key personal learning.

2. *Time-lines or life-lines.* These are adaptable exercises which can be used as listening exercises or to trigger pair or small group exchanges on a range of dimensions: attitudes, degree of learning, sense of progress, strength of feelings or assessment skills. For example, draw a line representing the present period of your life: when did it begin? when do you think it might end? Mark (a) the low spot during that period, (b) the high spot and (c) where you think you are now. If I were to do that exercise now, I would come up with:

July 1994----------------- a/---------- c/----- b/---------------April 1996.

For me that would represent a difficult period of family problems around health and work uncertainties, some of which should be clearer by April 1996; the sudden death of my much loved dog, Zinny, in February and serious damage to my back in the process (a); now, struggling against deadlines to finish this book (c), and the high spot of December when I hope it will be done (b)! Sharing and exploring those 'facts' with a partner would provide the possibility of much valuable insight into my present life-priorities, emotional responses and implications for my professional practice and development. Similar work can be done using the notion of transition (see Chapter 4) to identify the sequence of emotional reactions.

3. *Guided Imagery.* There are many exercises using relaxation and guided imagery which can produce much material for self-disclosure, empathic communication exercises or exploration of responses to theoretical, client or case material. They can involve self-evaluation (for example, ending a guided journey at a 'Magic Shop', which allows course members to choose one or more personal qualities they would like to develop and leave one or more behind which they like less about themselves); personal planning, linked with creative activity such as drawing (for example, draw a road map

of your journey through the course/the next two years); and pictorial or musical or movement representation of responses to stimulus material; or, perhaps most powerfully, images which surface for exploration and sharing in whatever way seems significant.

4. *Metaphors, similes, imagery*. Offering people a metaphor or image, or asking them to choose one, and then working with or exploring it in some way, can produce much material for considering events and perceptions within the course, individual responses or self-evaluation or explicit and implicit emotional and cognitive processes. For example, asking a group to consider themselves as an ocean liner (or a factory or on a desert island), allocate roles to themselves and/or other individuals within the group, explore the nature of the present voyage/product/shipwreck and the state of repair of the ship/business/coping strategies; this will produce much material for discussion, perception-checking and exploration in any combination of twos, small groups and the whole group. As with so many exercises, in addition to the feelings, interpersonal responses and attitudes in the moment, there will always be the likelihood of positive and negative projections, transference, counter-transference and other unconscious processes, or re-stimulated emotional and attitudinal material colouring or distorting the exchanges. Again, trainer clarity and ability are vital in managing the sensitive debriefing and untangling of such issues. These activities also provide immediate and very real opportunities for developing the core skills of communicating empathy, acceptance and genuineness; they will also parallel situations and issues which may arise with clients.

5. *Instruments, tests, inventories*. These are many and varied, for a range of purposes and acceptable or not to practitioners for a variety of reasons. As with all 'tests', such as personality inventories, check-lists, Myers-Briggs Type Indicators, the crucial training issue is how such triggers are used, what kind of opportunities they provide for structured activity followed by reflective exploration and how flexible they can be in application. They should provide stimulus rather than labelling and open up issues for exchange rather than close down options by prescriptive statements. Other creative stimuli, prompting similar 'sorting and sifting' of ideas, values and constructs can involve Tarot cards, Angel cards, pebbles, puppets or any other visual or pictorial material which invites participants to identify, make choices, compare or contrast themselves with others or with themselves at other life points. A key issue here is who has the ownership of the learning: activities which stay within the power of the trainee to make sense of or not as she is able are very different from tests which rely on interpretation by an external expert – and may have more potential for the individual's personal growth. This is a very different approach to that used traditionally by, for example, psychologists.

ADVANTAGES AND PROBLEMS OF STRUCTURED ACTIVITIES

Since this book is not intended to be a 'how to' manual, those examples must suffice of the kinds of specific structured activities which can be utilized in a course and some of the ways in which they might further personal awareness and development, whatever other primary purpose they are intended to fulfil. It is the trainer's task to keep a dual focus in all course activities: what learning is possible about 'x' (theory, skills, clients, ethics) and what learning is available about me/you, through the process of engagement with 'x'? There are, of course, complex issues when techniques such as guided imagery from psychosynthesis or scripts/slogan work from transactional analysis are removed from their origins and used for different purposes, separated from their root theory and conceptualization by trainers lacking understanding or imagination. There are dangers in an uninformed eclecticism, in inexperienced trainers using blindly activities which might have unintended consequences and negative effects for individuals or the course as a whole. Sufficient support must always be available if course members are triggered into distress of any sort; trainers need the skills and experience to distinguish between distress caused by ill-used stimulus material and sensitive emotional responses in individuals indicating significant areas for further personal work. There may, on the other hand, be a degree of protectionism from specialists wanting to intensify the mystique around their techniques and strategies, so that other trainers are discouraged from experimenting in creative ways with new approaches.

There are considerable advantages to using structured activities to further personal awareness and development. Increased sensitivity and responsiveness of course members to themselves and to each other generally mean, at best, as I suggested earlier:

- a warmth of climate
- positive relationships of trust
- reinforcement of helping skills and core qualities
- a high degree of bonding in the group
- the ability to focus and be concrete on specific personal examples
- an increase in openness and safety and therefore more willingness to take risks
- a greater understanding of clients
- improved skills of immediacy and self-disclosure
- clarification of attitudes, values, beliefs and constructs, which might help or impede work with clients
- a general reinforcement of communicating effectively about issues and processes that matter – hardly a handicap to counsellors!

It is important to note that there may be some problems in such structured activities with a double focus: whatever skill or issue is being explored plus personal awareness. Early on in any course trainees can be clumsy with each other, either ignoring or distorting significant personal material. They may inadvertently operate as a tin-opener, when the other person has insufficient time, support or control to avoid inappropriate distress. At times, trainees working in twos or threes can be collusive with each other in reinforcing or avoiding personal issues, or can forge intense personal pairings at a cost to group bonding and sharing. This can lead to 'splitting' in the larger group and make cohesiveness, trust and sharing much more difficult. Such work can be too trainer-dominated, especially early in a course, if all stimulus and processing of intra- and interpersonal awareness come from the trainer and her imposed structures. There is, though, a fine balance of trainer involvement: with too little, there is no way of monitoring the degree of distress or of learning course members may be experiencing, what inequalities of time and attention-taking there may be, or how far the core tasks, at both levels, are being achieved. Trainers' responses to these issues will also be related to their position on the trainer-directed–self-directed continuum, but they should react always to the particular needs of any group at any specific point in its history.

As with every aspect of course design, teaching and learning methods and personal development work, what matters most is the ability of trainers – and as the course progresses, the ability of trainees – to use sensitively their 'multi-lens spectacles' to work constantly with the *process* of experiences as well as the *content*, thus paralleling counsellor sensitivities and complexities with clients.

SKILLS

This chapter has outlined some of the methods and issues in trainee counsellors' work on personal development with other course members in a range of structured activities varying from skills practice through the exploration of metaphors and similes to the use of inventories and typologies such as Myers-Briggs. All these involve not only undertaking the exercises and tasks but also the communication and relationship skills needed to share with fellow participants both the experience of the activity itself and any learning which results from it. These skills are, of course, central in working with clients and so reinforced in this process. Pivotal in the learning from such structured activities are the abilities to reflect on experience, to notice and identify feelings, responses and sensations and to analyse (break down), synthesize (build up) and contextualize (apply) the elements of meaning and significance in any experience. These skills of reflection and identifying learning (or the gaps in it) are crucial for increasing counsellors' awareness in their work with clients, in supervision and, indeed, in making the most of all the potential learning from being in groups of all kinds which Chapter 9 will explore.

SOME QUESTIONS

1. Are there any limitations to the use of structured activities to promote personal development?

2. What training values underpin this way of working?

3. What criteria would you use to judge the appropriateness or timing of a particular exercise?

4. How do you balance the learning needs of trainees between skills and personal development?

5. How does a trainer decide what kind of exercises to use, and when?

6. As a trainer, do you ever abandon your planned activities with a group? On what grounds?

NINE

How do we do it (III)?

Personal development through groups

During any in-depth counselling training, participants are likely to have experience in a large group, (the whole learning community), smaller structured groups for skills learning and practice, supervision or support, and, depending on course rationale and philosophy, structured or unstructured groups specifically labelled as for personal development. Forests of trees have been sacrificed in attempting to describe, conceptualize, analyse and interpret the ways groups operate, different theoretical models, the range of facilitator styles, individual experiences and so on. The scope of this book precludes exploring in detail all those frameworks. This chapter will attempt to identify some of the salient issues concerning personal development. For more detailed exploration of group theory and group life, see Houston (1990), Smith (1980) and Vernelle (1994).

Why are groups important in counselling training and how do they contribute to personal development? One of the agreed central aims of training is to increase self-knowledge and self-acceptance, to enable participants to make visible to themselves their core assumptions and beliefs, values and attitudes. Those colour interactions with other people, relationships with clients, peers and colleagues, perceptions and feelings about the world and the meaning of life: they can only be fully revealed and tested in open comparison with others' attitudes, by responses and feedback from other people and by seeing and feeling how behaviour driven by our values directly affects and is perceived by other members of our world; hence, groups! Interpersonal exchanges are as vital in our development as intrapersonal exploration: both help us to make 'unconscious and subconscious assumptions conscious ... ' (Connor, 1994), a crucial element in personal and professional development as counsellors. Groups also provide many subtle contexts for us as developing counsellors to practise living out and deepening our capacity to communicate the core conditions; to assess our consistency and blindspots in being genuine, accepting and empathic; and to notice our ability to respond cognitively, affectively and through our behaviour to others who are communicating well or badly on the same dimensions. As a trainee at the end of his Diploma course reflected recently:

I feel so close now to most of the other members of the course – we've shared so many ups and downs. I have more sense of my own strength and can risk saying what I feel. I still have a vivid memory, though, of the first three months, when I saw myself as very different from everyone else – that was a lonely time.

Being in any group has gains and costs for most individuals. Gains can include:

- experiencing interactions with other people in very concrete and immediate ways, which can reinforce effective interpersonal patterns, challenge unhelpful ones and allow for possible changes to be tested out;
- reduce loneliness and isolation belonging to age and stage, life space or existential uncertainties by providing a supportive, bonded, at times loving, connection with peers in shared, purposeful activity;
- provide opportunities to see and feel the consequences of our projections of others;
- offer, in other group members, a range of alternative models of being, behaving and communicating which may assist in us loosening or even changing some of our own constructs and strait-jackets in feeling, thinking and acting.

On the other hand, in what Benson (1987) called the paradoxes and 'white-water rapids' of groupwork, the costs of group membership can involve painful feelings of exposure, vulnerability and anxiety. People can:

- feel excluded or scapegoated;
- suffer the insensitivities, righteous, relevant or inappropriate anger and clumsiness of others;
- feel unsafe and uncontained, overdependent on or hostile to peers or group leaders;
- feel bored, frustrated, impotent or critical of self and/or others.

Whether large or small, structured or unstructured, facilitated or leaderless, purposeful or anarchic, groups of any kind provide many experiences that have parallels with and relevance for counselling. It is impossible in groups to avoid issues of belonging and not belonging; limits, rules and boundaries; containment and safety – within which risks can perhaps be taken – or anxiety and fear; cohesion or conflict; dependence, independence and interdependence; and relationships ranging from a pragmatic working alliance to moments of closeness and intensity, of 'I–thou' experience within the group. Groups with different purposes allow for a range of experiences. For example, in a counselling group, leadership, intensity of feeling, degree of individual emotional work in depth will be very different than in a seminar discussion group. Similarly, any sharing of personal history will be less likely in a large learning community than in a small regular support group. The question of balance is crucial in all group experience: balance between task and process, between content and feelings, and crucially, between the overall function of the group, the needs of the whole membership and individual needs. Groups create a complex weave of literal and symbolic threads – more than the sum of their parts – and almost inevitably raise questions of cohesiveness, competition and conflict and how to deal with anxiety, frustration or helplessness.

LARGE GROUPS

What is the point of being in this group? We waste hours in silence, everybody gazing at the floor, waiting for something to happen! And some people seem to use the group as an excuse to attack and be unpleasant.

It is significant that many trainees report that their most frightening, uncomfortable and sometimes unusable experiences of groups is in (depending on the language of the course) the large group, the whole course, the learning community, while in contrast, much more safety, learning and positive challenge is claimed for small groups, whether structured and facilitated or not. All groups move through some evolving developmental process, in order to meet together, get to know each other, deal with conflicts, learn to work productively and find a way of ending – very like counselling itself! These processes – stages or cycles of activity – have been variously described by theorists such as Tuckman, Schutz, Bion and Randall and Southgate (see Vernelle, 1994). Any difficulties can seem magnified in large groups and therefore more frightening. What seems crucial for trainer understanding is that: (a) any theories are only models, notional conceptualizations, 'not the truth' about groups; (b) a great deal does happen all the time, however explained, in groups – between and within people, to do with 'here and now' factors and 'there and then' influences; and (c) all is magnified and feels less safe in large groups compared with smaller ones and it is harder for the facilitator to 'hold' the group and all its processes in the mind, so more destructive or disturbing behaviour may be possible, indeed likely.

There are interesting questions to be posed about conventional commitment in training to large group experience, particularly of an unstructured 'navel-gazing' kind; groups, like crowds or mobs, have potential for spinning out of control, for scapegoating and for frustration and fear. There is of course much to be learned from fear; and counsellors must know what frightens them. Yet, if the same learning potential is present in smaller groups with their generally greater safety as well as learning and risk, then it seems perverse (and philosophically inconsistent with core counselling values, certainly person-centred ones) to persist with a group experience which contains, at times, more anxiety, ambiguity and closing-down confrontation than creative learning opportunities. My challenge is, perhaps, to the assumption that large groups are particularly significant in counsellor training – an assumption that has its roots in earlier training or experiential models lost in the mists (or myths) of the 1960's encounter culture.

The complex layers of relationships, perceptions and (mis)-communications in large groups make it exponentially more difficult for individuals to check out the reality of their assumptions about other people and others' perception of and responses to them. Yet it is the whole group in any course which composes the learning community and provides the parameters of the course learning environment: it is in this group that the personal, social, creative and transpersonal energies of all the course participants will converge and transmute into collective and individual power or impotence. For positive outcomes, shared clarity of purpose for all participants, translated into clear working agreements or contracts (Proctor, 1991) and the joint endeavour of all to work for trust and openness, are essential. In such a climate, in however large or complex a group, individuals will be able to continue to learn about themselves in relation to a wide range of others and to understand other people better: key elements for counsellors in training.

Frameworks for conceptualizing large groups and their potential will be affected by any readers' or trainers' theoretical orientation. Psychodynamic interpretations, for example, can provide valuable insight into projections, defences, transferences, splitting, collusions, hostilities and generalizations. They can be, though, at best only a partial truth in such a complex whole, encourage ambivalent dependence on the interpreter/leader and reduce participants' confidence in their own 'making meaning' of the experience. In contrast, a person-centred model of working in the large group will emphasize all members' struggles for genuineness, empathy and congruence, may increase trust and acceptance, yet may find conflict and tension difficult to own and deal with. As ever, no one model or conceptualization can be 'the truth'; trainers, group facilitators or tutors who assume that group activity brings automatic benefits, who deny that groups, especially large groups, can do harm as well as good, can confirm anxieties and fears rather than reduce them, can distort rather than clarify, may limit the potential for personal development through groups rather than enhance it. The greatest risk, perhaps, is that the powerful and manipulative abilities which allow some members to over-dominate or block effective work in large groups, silencing others in the process, can frighten trainers too, paralyse their skills and promote an unhelpful climate characterized by tension, anxiety and negative self-interest. There is an inherent paradox in large groups that members will often want structure, yet fight for autonomy and dislike any rules.

It is of course in large groups that it is most difficult to balance and achieve task needs, whole group needs and individual needs: personal development is likely then to be limited. In some training philosophies there is a view that all business to do with groups should be kept for and dealt with in those groups, but for some individuals and some concerns it is helpful and valuable to have an opportunity to reflect on and explore them first in a safer space. Structuring pair or trio exchanges in support partnerships before and after large group; experience; encouraging reflexive learning in journal-keeping; taking issues to personal counselling before bringing them back to the group; and modelling disclosure can all allow group members to identify, address and work through personal issues and their application to development as counsellors.

A trainer's willingness and skills in communicating her responses openly, consistently and genuinely will help tackle the inevitable issues of leadership dependency and power/responsibility in the group, since much will be available for exploration in the moment. There is though a fine and difficult balance, especially in large groups, between trainers being willing to show both humility and vulnerability, yet still being seen as strong enough, 'good enough' and brave enough to hold and manage all the complexities of a large group of mature adults facing the challenges of learning, interpersonal and intrapersonal development. Some group members will be invested in competing for power and control with the leader/trainer and have old scripts and anger about unsatisfactory or unsafe parenting: trainer vulnerability and openness, however steeped in strength, is hard for them to handle and may be misread or abused. Trainers have needs as human beings, yet these issues of strength/vulnerability and genuineness/authority are at the heart of some of the most complex trainer tasks: core material for supervision and trainer personal development. A member of a Masters group expressed some of her confusion as follows:

When the trainer showed in the first term how upset she was, I felt in such a muddle. I really liked the way she was honest and didn't pretend to be unaffected by her mother's death. At the same time, I wanted her to be there fully for us, not have to protect her in any way – and an old bit of me (the critical part) felt she shouldn't have cried in the group.

Groups have a developmental life which is not necessarily linear, with some issues needing to be aired and explored over and over again, such as the struggle between flexibility and clear ground rules or the desire for autonomy and the need to be directed.

SMALL GROUPS

Most counselling training courses provide opportunities for a range of experiences in small groups, some task-focused and structured for skills practice or supervision or processing theory, some which may be structured or unstructured, specifically for personal development. Both kinds have great potential for furthering individual growth and relating personal issues to counselling theory, practice and process with clients.

Task-focused/structured small groups

Experience and some research (Kurtz, 1975) suggests that the more structured small groups are, whether trainer led or peer managed, the clearer the purpose and intentionality they will have, the more a task or tasks will be in focus and the easier trainees will find it at least to begin work in them! So groups for skills practice, supervision, seminars for processing theory, and even peer support groups will have a clear reason for meeting, a framework and context for activity and some expectations and control over group members' behaviour and contribution. There is likely to be some systematic approach to the tasks of such groups which will provide a degree of safety and purpose, helpful to some trainees in reducing the anxiety and uncertainties prevalent in less clearly-focused group activities. The expectations, controls, limits and structures provided may, paradoxically, make it easier for some members to engage at their own pace, to share personal responses and open up aspects of themselves more naturally to others, as if incidentally and certainly less self-consciously, alongside the main purpose of the group. Structure, clarity and safety can be freeing rather than constraining and provide firm ground for early steps in self-exploration and self-disclosure.

It is likely, too, that the task content of such groups will in itself provide opportunities for trainees to identify and work on aspects on themselves in their development as counsellors. It is helpful to use personal material in skills practice groups, stimulated by interactions with peers, responses to trainers, and reflections on life outside the course. For example, a trainee might explore any discomfort he experiences in sharing emotional responses with other men. Again, in supervision groups, early modelling and teaching by trainers can demonstrate that key issues for exploration may arise from individual counsellor responses, feelings and attitudes, at least as much as from facts about clients, interventions or theories. A recent instance involved a generally very accepting trainee, who was having great difficulty in allowing a vulnerable client autonomy and who was feeling inappropriately protective. It may be useful, too, in seminar/discussion groups where theory is in focus, to personalize and apply, for example concepts of human development or counselling psychology, to individual trainees' own history and present life, so that theory is made concrete and particular and the illustrative material and examples come from the richest resource of all – course members' own lives and understandings. For instance, transition theories and their implications for clients become vivid through considering current or recent transitions experienced by trainees.

However purposeful, relatively safe and therefore freeing such structured or task groups may be, individual and group processes will still be operating. The following central human dilemmas will all be present:

- wanting to be separate yet belong;
- longing for intimacy yet needing distance;
- feeling attraction for some people and antipathy to others;
- needing excitement and stimulus to learn, yet fearing risk and feeling caught by anxiety;
- wanting to change and grow while being defensive and resisting change;
- having needs yet not wanting to appear vulnerable.

People will learn and change, given adequate trust, a safe enough climate and receptive, responsive skills in others. Optimizing personal development for all members will depend, essentially, on three elements.

(i) *Preparing individuals for their contribution.* At the start of any counselling course, time should be spent on preparing participants to be clients for all the ensuing practical and skills work. Discussion might take place of appropriate levels of self disclosure for activities of different length or purposes; individuals can generate lists of possible topics/themes/issues with an indication of which would be easy to talk about, which is difficult to disclose (depending perhaps on the listener/counsellor) and which is out of bounds at least for now; and the beginning of self-scanning and monitoring encouraged on personal patterns of thinking, feeling and behaving, which are likely to be helpful or hindering in their new role of counsellor. A trainee on an introductory weekend offered this list (E = easy; D = difficult; O = out of bounds):

- anxiety about being a good enough counsellor(E)
- coping with essays(E)
- relationship with my partner(O)
- fears about unknown aspects of myself(D)
- feeling prejudiced against religion(D)
- sharing my values about being a 'helper'(E)
- an episode in my life I am ashamed of(O)
- sexual history(D).

Most trainers are familiar with course members at the beginning of training who deny having any personal concerns to explore: on the one hand, the course selection process must be questioned if this lasts for long, but on the other, some people have to learn to be self-reflective, to first bring into awareness, and then find ways of communicating issues of personal difficulty or intensity. We as trainers sometimes take this ability for granted, yet self revelation is hardly familiar or easy in, for example, British culture, where restraint, privacy and 'family business' are still powerful constructs.

(ii) *Encouraging a focus, from selection onwards, on process as well as content, feelings as well as facts,* and the encouragement of a culture of openness and support, challenging of self and others – of acknowledging subtexts, hidden agendas and exploration of shadow as well as sunlight.

(iii) *Teaching, learning and modelling by trainers of the core skills of active listening, self disclosure and direct communication.* These skills should then become the vehicle for all exchanges amongst members of the course community, all group members can make their contribution in a receptive and responsive climate and all can begin to trust and feel trustworthy.

Personal development groups

It is in small, usually unstructured, though facilitated groups that counselling training has traditionally cornered those opportunities for intra- and especially interpersonal exploration which have been seen as essential for the personal development of would-be counsellors. Those groups which in the early counselling training in Britain in the mid-1960s tended to be called T groups, encounter groups or sensitivity groups, acknowledged the significance of the person as counsellor, the ethical and professional importance of self-knowledge, and the paramount need for self- and other-awareness in the conduct of any counselling relationship. The purpose is both to enhance the therapeutic potential for any client and to guard against abuse and manipulation for the counsellor's needs rather than the client's. The movement more recently in counselling training to term these 'personal development' groups reflects perhaps some greater clarity about purpose – although trainees often find it notoriously difficult on many courses to understand the rationale and intention embedded in such groups. There seems often some gap between trainer intention and actuality!

'Development' implies learning and potential change and reminds us that trainees on a course are engaged essentially in a learning process, while 'personal' reiterates that the self of the counsellor and the personal relationship implemented by that self are crucial to the effectiveness of any counselling exchange. There are three main elements in the rationale for such focused groups:

- so much is triggered for mature adults facing all the transitions of self-

perception, role and attitude in becoming trainees/learners, the
process of which will provide a roller-coaster of experience;

- working with clients' material will inevitably stimulate thought, feeling and behaviour responses, not all of which will be acceptable or easy to manage;
- every aspect of life, inside and outside the course, all the unplanned life events and existential questions, will be affecting individuals, their ways of being with themselves and with others.

This is likely to be particularly marked since trainees will be developing a heightened awareness and sensitivity. It is the facilitator's task to create a (comparatively) safe space, to 'hold the boundaries' of the group, to clarify and promote both individual and group needs, and to be clear about the purpose and process of the group and her own role within it. All participants should agree to engage in interpersonal exchange and mutual feedback, while the group members must agree to be self-reflective about their experiences on the course and outside it, their strengths and difficulties, their personal patterns, values, attitudes and assumptions. These emerge as they deepen their understanding and practice of counselling through their work on the course, their interaction with fellow trainees, trainers and colleagues elsewhere and their engagement with clients.

There is general agreement (although it is much easier to state in theory than to manage in practice) that such a group is not a therapy group. Sometimes deep feelings will be triggered and expressed and personal work may begin, which will then need to be taken elsewhere (for example, to personal counselling) for more in-depth work. In a recent personal development group:

> *An ex-nurse explored issues around a struggle for power between another member and the facilitator. There was much to work on in the group around authority relationships, implicit and explicit control, relevant to her as a counsellor. There was, then, also a degree of distress, which seemed to cloak fear rooted in some family pattern that she noted and took to her own counselling.*

It is a paradox that in such a comparatively safe group, some members will be resistant and some will want to work in much greater therapeutic depth than is deemed appropriate: the constant questions for facilitator and members are around: how deep? how far? how much attention to one or more individuals? how appropriate is this issue/depth/focus? They are always difficult questions to answer and there are rarely absolute answers. As ever the response is about balance and context: balance of time, attention and response, shared amongst all the group members in the context of learning to be a counsellor. The personal development group is not a place for intensive personality restructuring or therapeutic work on and for one individual at the expense of all other members; rather it is a key forum for sharing and processing all aspects of personal learning and interpersonal interaction as they occur in the group and elsewhere on the course.

The theoretical orientation of any trainer and the core values of a course may be highly relevant here: in a course run on psychodynamic principles, unconscious processes and, in particular, transference relationships are likely to be high profile and the style/role of the facilitator will need to be appropriate and appropriately distant. In contrast, in a person-centred course, the primary emphasis is likely to be on genuineness, congruence and the skills of self-disclosure and immediacy, with the facilitator modelling the skills and entering as fully as possible into the process of the group, while being clear and open about the similarities and differences between her role and those of the group members. These two orientations can be captured, perhaps, in the very different facilitator styles which ensue: the psychodynamic trainer is likely to use interpretation and observation at a distance, while the-person-centred facilitator may verbalize her awareness and understanding of the group or individual processes she experiences while acknowledging her part in them in the moment. There are of course dangers and limitations in all approaches. The right to interpret should be earned and, when ill-timed, too absolute or inaccurate, can sometimes destroy or disable the natural process of the group; congruence and genuineness in a facilitator can be construed as weakness, vulnerability or being partisan. Of crucial importance – and now generally agreed – is that the style and theoretical orientation of the personal development group and group facilitators should match the core values of the course or at least be not in opposition. They should certainly be consistent over time. If this is not the case, trainees experience considerable confusion and dissonance which is a distraction rather than an enhancement of their personal learning. Some kind of splitting is almost always another consequence: course good, facilitator bad or the reverse! In reality, of course, even within any one orientation, there will be individual facilitator differences as a consequence of belief, values and personality; part of trainee development is to understand, accept and work with those differences.

There are a number of other issues in relation to personal development groups which I must attempt to highlight. These include interlinked questions of (i) contracting and confidentiality; (ii) group membership and continuity; (iii) facilitation (who and how) and assessment; (iv) structure and content; and (v) any group contribution to the support–challenge continuum and to the balance of pain and gain in group learning. If personal development, the acknowledgement, processing, and sharing of strengths, limitations and vulnerabilities, is accepted as part of all course activities, then differentiation between what happens in the personal development group and elsewhere becomes much less significant; the group becomes merely another (if valuable) mechanism for promoting personal learning.

(i) *Contracting and confidentiality*. As was emphasized earlier, clarity of purpose in personal development groups is essential and can be attempted (though not always achieved) by clear information and intention being stated to a course group on paper and verbally; opportunity provided for clarification and discussion; then a contracting process undertaken in which facilitators and group members share their understanding of, acceptance of and agreement to the tasks and methods of the group. An example from a Diploma course includes the following statement for discussion at the start of a new group:

The group is to provide opportunities for:

- Exploration of personal and interpersonal process in relation to being on the course and becoming a counsellor
- Examining personal assumptions, attitudes, patterns and responses as they arise with peers, staff, clients and others
- Identifying blind spots and vulnerabilities which may then be taken elsewhere for further exploration
- Learning to be self-reflective about strengths and limitations
- Developing the capacity to respond attentively to and learn from others.

Some trainers – in a half-understood commitment to experiential learning – feel discomfort in explaining in advance the potential purposes of this area of training in case it forecloses on student choices and precludes discoveries. My own value is that *not* to share what I know or think I know is to keep power to myself as trainer and to manipulate trainees in a potentially irresponsible manner. This is, indeed, a central question in experiential learning: to balance the provision of opportunities for self-discovery and new learning with the anxiety and sense of being manipulated in some trainees when available information is not shared by trainers in advance of experiences perceived as difficult. A secondary issue is that contracting has to take place at or near the beginning of a group's life, when participants may be so anxious or lacking in understanding that they are unable fully to comprehend what is involved. As with so many aspects of learning, the contracting process must be regularly revisited and the outcomes renegotiated. As part of this process the relationship has to be made clear between work and personal sharing undertaken in the small group and the rest of the course – amongst other large group members, tutors, one-to-one work outside the small group and so on. Very often, confidentiality in a training course is more of an issue in theory than reality: it becomes less significant between one part of a course and another if there is an overall climate of trust, if individuals feel respected and not abused, and if genuineness and self disclosure are core course values. However, trust has to be earned and the need to thrash out issues, anxieties and fantasies about confidentiality is often very strong in some individuals; it may indicate a high level of anxiety and insecurity which can be assuaged by full discussion in order to release energy for learning, which may otherwise stay blocked. Time spent at the beginning of a group on agreeing ground rules, checking assumptions and acknowledging limits and difficulties will be well spent. Such ground rules can be very simple if they are designed and/or agreed with the group; a recent Masters course I worked with settled for the following:

- Be respectful; don't gossip;
- Respect anonymity outside the group;
- It is OK to make mistakes;
- It is OK to change;
- It is OK to say what we need;
- Keep agreed time boundaries;
- Say I.

(ii) *Group membership and continuity.* Most Diploma and Masters level courses operate with a course group of between sixteen and thirty members. Unless a decision is made that all personal development will take place specifically in the whole group (unusual these days, though not unknown in earlier training models), smaller groups will have to be created. The central issues here are whether members of a small personal development group stay constant over the whole life of a course, how they get into that group in the first place and all the related questions of power, choice and emotional responses. The three main models of creating small personal development groups (by custom and practice about eight to twelve members) are: *allocation by tutors* on predetermined criteria, which would usually involve aiming for a mixed group, balanced in terms of, for example, gender, age, working context, sexual orientation, and/or culture/ethnicity; a range of *random methods of allocation* such as numbering around a large group, then all the 'ones' go together, all the 'twos' and so on, alphabetical lists divided off into eights, colour choices and so on; and, thirdly, inviting the large group to *choose/sort themselves* into groups of eight, either with base criteria given or the group being first asked to reach consensus on the criteria they are going to use. Each method, from my experience, is equally likely to produce an effective/disabled working group! Each produces, potentially, anger of different kinds – at tutor power, at the unfairness of random fate or at other people for choosing/not choosing them, and each method has advantages and costs. Essentially, the work of the groups will begin at a different point, although will then cover much of the same ground, depending on which method is selected. Power and responsibility are key issues in all methods, but are located differently. If the third, trainee choice method is adopted, the course members have to face very early in a course their own responsibilities for taking or avoiding decisions, the consequences of owning attractions and pairings with some peers, facing or avoiding antipathy with others. Primitive feelings of inclusion and rejection are triggered, which can cloak other concerns or raise unhelpfully high anxiety.

Yet, just as in counselling itself, individuals have to begin to recognize their own thoughts and feelings, tackle or evade choices and live with the consequences, planned and unintended of their actions. If this process happens right at the start of the course, people will have little real sense of each other so will be operating on instinct, projections, fantasies, attribution, echoes of significant people in their earlier lives and so on. This provides much early material for the group to work on but is clearly different than choices made later in the course life when participants have begun to know each other better. There are also complex issues which arise if some members of the large group already know each other in other capacities or have been members of earlier courses. It may then be important to include in the criteria positive or at least non-negative criteria such as age or experience or geographical area and criteria to avoid, such as previous knowledge or contact. In contrast, tutor or random allocation can allow a safer passage into the new small group, without such sharply focused and highly visible anxiety in choices; at the same time, fantasies of trainer power, motivation and hidden agendas can be stimulated by all but the most glaring randomization – and even then, the 'fickle finger of fate' can arouse feelings of being a victim, if the resulting group membership is not appealing or acceptable. Pairing facilitators with groups – whether chosen by the group or allocated randomly or by predetermined criteria – raises the same range of issues and potential for anger, anxiety, disappointment or excitement.

Continuity, membership of the same group over the duration of the course or reshuffling after, for example, the first year, raises questions of depth versus variety. A group whose members come to know each other very well over the whole length of a course has a spiral curriculum of the same intra- and interpersonal issues revisited over two or three years, with different depths and meanings, interleaved with new learning. In contrast, if the groups re-form, there is more chance of meeting in some, though less depth, a greater variety of peers with the benefit of more than one (preferably different) experience of choosing, beginning and performing in a newly directed group. Since the opportunity of being in a personal development group is rare in life, the depth and continuity option is probably most valuable, since professional and personal life offers other opportunities of joining groups more frequently though at less depth. A similar question applies to whether a group stays with the same facilitator for its whole life: I take the opposite view to the group membership option – exposure to more than one style of facilitation can offer helpful learning.

(iii) *Facilitation (who and how) and assessment.* Personal development groups are generally viewed as central in many models of counselling training. In order to optimize the potential for trainee learning it is almost invariably seen as important that they are facilitated by experienced group leaders. There are, however, some key questions for any trainer responsible for course design: how does the facilitator understand her role and function; what theoretical orientation is most helpful; what facilitation styles are appropriate; and, perhaps most contentiously, should the facilitators be members of the core teaching/tutoring staff of the course or outsiders whose only contact with the course is this particular group. There are some relatively concrete answers to all but the last of those questions. The facilitator's role is:

- to create a safe learning space;
- to enable participants to take some risks in learning about themselves and others;
- to hold the group in her mind;
- to be alert to destructive group processes such as scapegoating, splitting and damaging individual behaviour;
- to monitor and stimulate the pace of movement of the group and individuals within it;
- to model appropriate skills of communication and interpersonal relating;
- to understand the learning needs of the group and assess its degree of sophistication and readiness for different phases of work;
- to be clear about the purpose of the group – development not therapy, self-awareness not self-indulgent narcissism, learning to be a counsellor not vague personal growth;
- to be clear about her responsibilities within it: to create a group climate which optimizes member involvement, trust and a 'working' culture.

Within those functions, styles of facilitation will vary according to the task and process needs of the group, the focus of work underway and the phase of group development. Clarity of information giving and outlining of group purpose are important at the start of any personal development group when the facilitator needs to create some security in the midst of inevitable uncertainty. A more negotiating, student-centred approach will be more appropriate when the group is established and members are more confident in taking their own power and control. The ability to distinguish which style is appropriate is a core trainer skill. Whatever variation in facilitator styles is relevant to the life of the group, the facilitator must be consistent (within the limits of theoretical orientation) in modelling active listening skills to communicate empathy, acceptance and genuineness and so build relationships. The facilitator also needs the capacity for openness and appropriate self-disclosure, receptiveness and clarity about any individual material relevant for the group, the ability to comment on and highlight group and individual process and the sensitivity and strength to manage painful issues, tensions, conflict in the group and, of course, its ending.

Theoretical orientation. It seems most helpful, in promoting learning and development, if both the facilitator's style and her theoretical orientation are the same as or in close accord with the principal orientation of the course as a whole. Orientations which appear to clash either in core values or in techniques may cause dissonance and confusion for trainees, especially early in their training. When counsellors are well established and experienced there is of course much to learn from being exposed to different models and approaches. For example, in Diploma and Masters courses few trainees are sufficiently experienced to manage the muddles which can arise. The relatively silent, interpretative manner of a psychodynamic facilitator, focusing on transference and unconscious defences, sits uneasily (and provokes much trainee anger and frustration) in a predominately person-centred course, otherwise modelling congruence, transparency and genuine self-disclosure. However ultimately learningful that anger and frustration might be, there are other ways, more consistent with the core model and less costly in ill-timed conflict, to explore the issues of ambiguity, uncertainty and anxiety, which are often present, especially at the start of a group. Since the core function of the personal development group is for trainees to extrapolate intra- and interpersonal learning of relevance to themselves as counsellors, it makes little sense for their conceptualizing of experiences in the group to be very different from their core counselling model and way of working with clients. As ever, insights from different models of counselling and group process may be valuable in deepening understanding, once a sufficiently sophisticated level has been reached of integration of theory and practice in the core training model.

Core staff or outsiders? Perhaps the most contentious issue is whether facilitators for personal development groups should be members of the core course staff or outsiders who have no other contact with the course. Much heat and little light is often expended on this question, which seems to rouse more passion and 'absolutism' than any other training issue. There is, as ever, a case to be made for both versions and much depends on the core values underpinning each view. Many of us would argue that personal development is so central that if core staff are not involved in personal development groups the activity is marginalized; trainers can, to an extent, evade responsibility for working intimately with trainees' strengths and limitations in a developmental way. Accepting the centrality of this part of trainee development then has implications for the nature and quality of trainer/trainee relationships. They will need to be cooperative and open rather than authoritarian and distant, if conflicts which arise are to be resolved constructively with the group. Person-centred practitioners, in particular, believe that if there is trust, acceptance and openness from all participants, then any difficult issues or differences of response which arise between trainer and trainees are part of the work of the group and the very material of learning from the group experience. Again, if core staff are involved in personal development groups, they can model genuineness and appropriate self-disclosure, demonstrating the skills of immediacy and participation, facing rather than evading any issues of interpersonal difficulty as they arise: all very important elements of being a counsellor. Staff need to know, too, the potential distress any trainee might be facing, in order to respond appropriately elsewhere in the course and they also have to know – and this is the rub for many who dispute trainer involvement – the limits of competence any trainee demonstrates, in self-awareness, non-defensiveness, willingness and ability to be self-reflective and take feedback from others.

Assessment. It is indeed around assessment, making judgements about trainees, that the arguments centre for those who believe that the personal development group facilitators should be separate from all the course activities. They argue that work in those groups should not be included in assessment, that trainees will then feel freer to bring the 'difficult' parts of themselves. This is very much the view of those who see boundaries of function and confidentiality as particularly important and who view the trainer role as synonymous with being an authority figure. Trainers with these beliefs see the outside facilitator as 'cleaner', less partisan and therefore less oppressive for trainees who might otherwise feel inhibited and need to hide their vulnerabilities and blind spots. Psychodynamic practitioners and those whose understanding of groups is primarily based on unconscious processes would also rate this model more highly because of the transference relationships around authority. There may indeed be potential difficulties or conflicts around roles, authority and judgement, yet, in my view, trainers and trainees must face the inevitability of assessment and evaluation if standards for professional counsellors are in focus. If we remember that the primary purpose of personal development groups is to increase the awareness and interpersonal skills of counsellors-in-training, not to operate as self-contained personal growth groups and certainly not primarily as therapy groups – then the role of the facilitators perhaps becomes clearer. Similarly, if personal development is in focus throughout all course activities, then the concern for arbitrary boundaries and separation of different kinds of learning opportunities and of assessment becomes irrelevant. An even stronger argument for core staff being involved as facilitators comes into play if trainers see their role as sharing with or giving away skills to trainees: as the group develops, then facilitation will gradually be shared by trainees and the experience of assessment too can be changed if self and peer assessment and evaluation are given adequate status. Formal assessment of personal development, in the shape of grades or marks is inappropriate, but questions and judgements for trainee counsellors around 'good enough' standards of self-awareness and interpersonal relationships seem unavoidable, if difficult and delicate. At the heart of all issues of facilitation and group membership must be the recognition that trainees are engaged in a developmental journey, are in the process of becoming counsellors; assessment and evaluation are then in the service of learning and growth, to be embraced (however tentatively) and not feared.

(iv) *Structure and content*. Many trainers seem committed to the assumption that personal development groups should be unstructured, that only then can individuals' conscious and unconscious needs, processes and issues be addressed, and only then can a truly trainee-centred focus be sustained. This view seems to beg the question of whether it is even possible to have, in real terms, an unstructured group, since the facilitator, at least, will have explicit and implicit expectations, reinforced by endless theories of groups and group work, of what processes and patterns will emerge. Much research in the 1970s (Vernelle, 1994) emphasized that some structure, for example specific invitations or exercises at the start of a group (both developmentally in its history and at the beginning of sessions), produced more cohesive groups, more engaged participants, more self-defined learning, a more positive view of facilitators and a higher level of interpersonal trust. Such structured activities ensure that everyone is included (for example, inviting everyone to make an opening or a closing statement), removes some of the (sometimes agonising) decisions about when and if to speak and eases group members into interaction early in a group's life when ambivalence and anxiety are strongest about its function, value and safety.

Counter-arguments emphasize possible overdependence on the leader/ facilitator, argue that structure moves the group members' focus out of the 'here and now' and suggest that key learning opportunities about individual patterns may be missed (for example, in an unstructured group, someone who manages not to speak at all is faced with the question of what stopped him or her). These objections perhaps lose sight of the fact that facilitation in the sense of suggesting starting activities can be shared by group members; that the debriefing of exercises is the crucial process for exploring intra- or interpersonal issues in the moment and that, following on from structured activities, modelling and encouraging reflective skills may be where the most important learning lies. Clearly, any trainer's theoretical orientation and training philosophy will influence her position on this question: perhaps the most important issues are firstly, to differentiate between a group's needs at its inception and later in its life and secondly, to ensure that trainees experience a range of approaches to optimize different kinds of learning. All counsellors-in-training need, at some stage, to experience uncertainty, ambivalence, and resistance which reflect aspects of work with clients and which can arise so powerfully in an unstructured group. My own view is that they will learn more effectively about those issues if some trust, security and purposeful closeness already exists. Similarly, I believe the key issues of intra- and interpersonal awareness of trainee counsellors – around their capacity for intimacy and separateness, their attitudes and prejudices, their blind spots and vulnerabilities, attractions and antipathies – can be identified and explored in different ways through both structured and unstructured processes.

(v) *Support and challenge, pain and gain?* Finally, the preceding section raises a central issue in the management and understanding of personal development groups: the need for a balance of support and challenge; the relationship between 'pain and gain'; and the difference in training philosophies which emphasize anxiety and uncertainty as fertile learning contexts compared with those which stress the need for trust, warmth and empathy. Trainers tend to cling to the wreckage of one or other of these approaches as if 'truth' was enshrined therein; certain kinds of learning experience have taken on the status of myth, linked implicitly though rarely explicitly, with core concepts and values from different theoretical orientations. So, unstructured, anxiety-provoking group experiences, understood through psychodynamic concepts and insights, with a distant, interpretative facilitator are artificially contrasted with trusting, supportive and potentially cosy person-centred groups with an open, self-disclosing facilitator: neither is the whole truth. Person-centred groups or groups based on gestalt, transactional analysis or psychodrama can be confronting and painful while psychodynamic groups can be safe containers for much valuable learning and emotional catharsis. As Vernelle (1994) stresses, the key in tapping the potential for learning in personal development groups, the central and most valuable relationship, is that between support and challenge. As in counselling, all evidence suggests that if adequate support and empathic acceptance are present, challenge can be creative, purposeful and effective in helping people change or change their view of themselves or others. Group experience can then contribute, paradoxically, to an increase in self-responsibility and most of all in self-esteem. Again, as earlier and later sections of this chapter try to demonstrate, personal development groups will be only one arena – but perhaps a crucial one – where such significant aspects of a counsellor-in-training will flourish.

Groups and learning styles

All groups, large, small, structured, unstructured, facilitated or peer-run can contribute to personal development in a number of ways. Individuals' learning is likely to be affected by:

- the roles people take or are sent (for example, the joker, clown or humorist in any group may help or hinder her own or others' learning);
- reactions to, for example, interpersonal feedback (someone who becomes instantly defensive at anything perceived as criticism is going to close down quickly);
- needs for status or contrast with status outside the group/course (for example, a priest who was used to unquestioning devotion from his parishioners in a small country parish);
- group pressure to conform or deviate from course norms (for

instance, in one personal development group many years ago, the men always arrived breathless having played football in the tea break – very isolating for the one man who separated himself from that activity).

Other pertinent issues which will affect learning include individuals' attitudes to authority and capacity for intimacy and closeness; hidden agendas (for example, conscious or unconscious antagonism towards the facilitator or one of the co-trainers); previous experience in groups; and other reference groups, past or present, which have shaped participants' understanding of or response to group involvement. Some course members with memories of earlier exciting experiences in growth or encounter groups approach groups in counselling training with an over-excited adrenaline-buzzing charge – which can be frustrating for themselves and/or frightening for others if the pace and focus of the personal development group is different. Again, if participants have experienced an in-depth therapy group, then the learning and development group in the context of becoming a counsellor may seem, especially at first, lukewarm and limited. In contrast, if group members' other experience is only of work groups, discussion groups or seminars, they will have little understanding of the intensity of concrete interpersonal feedback and the power of genuine self-disclosure.

Not everyone will learn and grow effectively in groups. A recent study of group work in counselling training (Irving and Williams, 1995) interestingly compared responses to and benefits from groups with different learning styles, based on the work of Honey and Mumford (1986). They outlined four preferred learning styles:

- *Activists* – engross themselves in the here and now and enjoy games and teamwork;
- *Reflectors* – stand back from events and think before acting;
- *Theorists* – learn best when situations have purpose and are stimulated when what they are doing is seen as part of something else;
- *Pragmatists* – concentrate on practical issues and like to see a link between what they learn and how they can use it.

Irving and Williams compared attitudes to group work with those learning styles and found some significant differences in perceptions, experiences, enthusiasm and attitude. For instance, those preferring to 'do' (activists and pragmatists) were more positive about the work than those preferring to 'think', (theorists and reflectors). Theorists and reflectors needed to know more about the purpose of the activity while activists just get on with it; pragmatists are talkative at the beginning and maintain a high emotional level throughout, while theorists are anxious at the start but feel safe at the end; reflectors are less confident and more intellectual at the beginning and become even less challenging by the end. All felt they had gained in personal development and self-awareness but saw what they had learned differently: for example, activists emphasized skills learning while reflectors noticed process as well as outcome. All but the pragmatists felt vulnerable and experienced some pressure and threat, though only activists thought groups might be destructive. All emphasized their need for help and support from others while reflectors and theorists saw confrontation as a pressure rather than an encouragement to participate, and so on.

In general, in this study, participants with all learning styles were ambivalent about group work, with little enthusiasm – although acknowledging its importance in development. This should raise some salutary questions for trainers who assume (a) that personal development should or must 'happen' in a group, and (b) that groups offer the same learning potential for all members. It seems, from this small study, reinforced by my own experiences of feedback from trainees, that not all individuals like or will benefit from group work, that individuals with different learning styles will need different facilitator approaches and will learn from different balances of support and challenge. It seems clear though that support and a climate of trust are always vital in all kinds of groups and for all individual learning styles.

As ever, there is no one source of truth or learning, especially in personal development. Groups have great potential as a forum for learning about ourselves and they also have limitations. Every person has individual learning needs with unique patterns of advantages and difficulties. It is all the more important then to see personal development as pervading and triggered by all activities in a counselling training course, all tasks and all combinations of participants, in order to promote Rogers' (1961) aims:

- the individual's efforts to become himself
- openness to experience
- trust in one's organism
- an internal locus of evaluation
- and the willingness to be a process.

SOME QUESTIONS

1. Is any experience in groups *unhelpful* in counselling training?

2. What can people learn from large groups?

3. Do structure or a task focus diminish or optimize personal development?

4. How does allegiance to any theoretical orientation affect facilitation?

5. Does your learning style (or styles) enhance your participation in groups?

TEN

Conclusion

'To get you have to give ... '?

In our finite, physical lives, we may run out of time for personal growth; similarly, I have little space left to outline some concepts helpful for framing personal development in counselling training. I want to draw attention to the context of it all and to some of the challenges I see as significant.

Just as counselling itself is much more than technical problem solving, so training in the field of counselling should not be a narrow, mechanistic process, but must fulfill the broader educational needs of the person who commits herself to it. I cannot engage here in a sterile debate about the differences, but instead wish to endorse the contribution that each – training and education – makes to the development of a rounded person and counsellor, to head and heart, intellect and emotion, mind and body. Knowledge, skills and awareness are all essential to an effectively functioning counsellor. That awareness, emphasized throughout the book, must ensure that we look outwards at the world around us, as well as inwards at our own needs, fears and abilities. Emmy van Deurzen-Smith (1993) has argued that an unquestioned drive for change – personal, social or technological – has costs as well as gains; that we must value too the 'hub of enduring sameness that can be found at the centre of the wheel of change'; and that the 'secular religion of counselling ... in which we preach self-improvement and a fierce absorption in the personal' has both limits and potential dangers, if it means that we are blind to wider existential and ecological issues. Change is not necessarily progress and may involve exploitation of others or of human resources. Consequences may include much that is positive, but also pain, loss, confusion, regret, selfishness or threat – not to be lightly unleashed.

I have argued that personal development is at the heart of becoming a counsellor: if it involves commitment not only to the individual but to a wider social and environmental context, that is a huge responsibility for trainers and trainees to undertake. Yet, greater awareness and sensitivity will almost inevitably embrace acceptance of the limitations of human control, both of ourselves and our universe, the inconsistencies which govern our lives and the need in our society for more positive emotional exchange to create a better climate for mental health and human relationships. Three concepts, then, which frame for me the journey of personal development are *chaos, paradox* and *ecology*. The following brief outline may raise some interesting questions.

Wolinsky (1994) has used the arguments of quantum physics to demonstrate that everything is connected to everything else, and that *chaos*, a principle of the universe, also operates in but is mostly resisted by human beings. He argues that the resulting wasted energy could be better used – and that order in life can come – by 'riding the rapids of chaos', rather than by fighting the feelings of being out of control and at the mercy of the apparent randomness of life. Instead of seeking causes, reasons, purposes of the pain, turbulence or confusions of human life, we might more usefully, he argues, accept the process and allow the chaos to order itself, so revealing deeper connections and meanings, and, most of all, putting us in touch with a free flow of energy, within us, between us and others and with the universe. How far this metaphor or model appeals to you will depend on values and belief systems; it has the merit of reminding me of my core belief in the inter-connectedness of things, even if I am uncertain how far along Wolinsky's path I can travel and what the implications might be for personal development.

Another convincing framework which allows considerable exploration of many issues is the concept of *paradox*, as an illuminating key to meaning. Throughout this book, I have touched on a number of paradoxes in personal development, which trigger questions and key issues. Handy's (1994) 'empty raincoat' is a symbol of the potential emptiness of our lives at the end of the twentieth century and of our struggle (central in personal development) to balance the contradictions and inconsistencies we experience. He offers nine 'paradoxes of our times': the Paradox of Intelligence, of Work, of Productivity, of Time, of Riches, of Organizations, of Age, of the Individual, and of Justice. All are relevant, some particularly so for counsellors-in-training. For example, The Paradox of Work reminds us that some of us have too much work, while others have too little, with the reverse true of so-called leisure; the Paradox of the Individual outlines both the need to belong and to be alone and emphasizes the alienation of the Internet or the 'virtual organization'; and the paradox of Age indicates that each generation sees itself as different from its predecessor, yet plans as if the next generation will be the same. Handy offers three metaphors for redesigning our lives in order to live more effectively in the realities of the present economic and political world: the Sigmoid Curve (the letter 'S' on its side, representing natural processes of waxing and waning), which involves taking risks in moving on while retaining some balance with what has gone before; the inside-out doughnut, a way of describing modern life as a filled core (of common interests and obligations) and a bounded space in our personal and working lives; and the Chinese contract, which necessitates compromise and 'win–win' outcomes. Both the paradoxes and the principles contained in Handy's images offer much of value to stimulate thinking about personal development.

The concepts of chaos and paradox remind us of inter-connectedness of all kinds; my third framework, that of *ecology*, similarly emphasizes the symbiotic relationships amongst people and between us and the universe, physical, cognitive and emotional. We affect each other in ways recognized and unknown; deliberate good or hurt as much as unintended consequences alike cause unavoidable ripples in the still or turbulent pond of our existence. There are moral and ethical questions about the purpose, power and potential of personal development: how can we ensure that all the energy, commitment and skill expended in counselling training produce concerned, compassionate practitioners of integrity and not 'little monsters' of selfishness? The slogan 'The personal is political' may be a key, if it reminds us that counselling – and counselling training – is about more than individual gratification. Counsellors and trainers must attend to the relationships, systems and networks in which people exist and which they could influence, if they choose.

Finally, counsellors and counsellors in training are human beings who can perhaps learn to operate with a level of 'emotional literacy' which, at best, might serve as a model for other relationships. Ideally, they might act as flag-bearers in raising standards of communication and interpersonal interaction, whatever the difficulties and stresses in society, which could improve the ecology of human experience. Grandiosity, as I stressed earlier, is not a helpful trait for counsellors; I shall settle, then, for Peter Daws' (1982) hope for counselling – and mine for personal development in counselling training – as:

'an optimistic creed for a pessimistic world'.

References

Allman, P. (1983) The Nature and Process of Adult Development. In M. Tight (ed.), *Education for Adults*. London: Croom Helm/Open University.

Annand, J.B. (ed.) (1977) *Education for Self-Discovery*. London: Hodder and Stoughton.

Assagioli, R. (1975) *Psychosynthesis*. New York: Turnstone Press.

Aveline, M.O. (1990) The training and supervision of individual therapist. In W. Dryden (ed.), *Individual Therapy: A Handbook*. Milton Keynes: Open University Press.

Benson, J.F. (1987) *Working More Creatively in Groups*. London: Routledge.

Berman, J. (1994) *Diaries to an English Professor*. Amherst: University of Massachusetts Press.

Bolger, A.W. (1982) *Counselling in Britain: A Reader*. London: Batsford.

Bond, T. (1993) *Standards and Ethics for Counselling in Action*. London: Sage.

Bridges, W. (1933) *Transitions*. Reading, Mass.: Addison-Wesley.

BAC (1990) *The Recognition of Counsellor Training Courses*. Rugby: British Association for Counselling.

BAC (1992/1994) *Code of Ethics and Practice for Counsellors*. Rugby: British Association for Counselling.

BAC (1995a) *Code of Ethics and Practice for Trainers*. Rugby: British Association for Counselling.

BAC (1995b) *Code of Ethics and Practice for Supervisors of Counsellors*. Rugby: British Association for Counselling.

British Psychological Society (1995) *Regulations and Syllabus for the Diploma in Counselling Psychology*. Leicester: British Psychological Society.

Bruner, J. (1986) *Actual Minds, Possible Worlds*. Cambridge, Mass.: Harvard University Press.

Campbell, D.P. (1974) *If you don't know where you are going, you'll probably end up somewhere else ...* Illinois: Argus Communication.

Casement, P. (1985) *On Learning from the Patient.* London: Tavistock.

Clark, N. (1991) *Managing Personal Learning and Change.* London: McGraw Hill.

Combs, A.W. (1986) What makes a good helper? *Person Centered Review* 1 51–61.

Connor, M. (1994) *Training the Counsellor.* London: Routledge.

Cox, M. and Theilgaard, A. (1994) *Shakespeare as Prompter.* London: Jessica Kingsley.

Dainow, S. and Bailey, C. (1988) *Developing Skills with People.* Chichester: Wiley.

Daws, P. (1982) Mental Health and Education: counselling as prophylaxis. In A.W. Bolger, *Counselling in Britain.* London: Batsford.

Dryden, W. (1991) *Dryden on Counselling Vol.1 Seminal Papers.* London: Whurr.

Dryden, W. (ed.) (1992) *Hard-Earned Lessons from Counselling in Action.* London: Sage.

Dryden, W. and Feltham C. (1994) *Developing Counsellor Training.* London: Sage.

Dryden, W. and Thorne, B. (eds) (1991) *Training and Supervision for Counselling in Action.* London: Sage.

Dryden, W., Horton, I. and Mearns, D. (1995) *Issues in Professional Counsellor Training.* London: Cassell.

Egan, G. (1973) *Face to Face.* Monterey: Brooks/Cole.

Egan, G. (1986, Third edition) *The Skilled Helper.* Monterey: Brooks/Cole.

Egan, G. and Cowan, M.A. (1979) *People in Systems: A model for Development in the Human-Service Professions and Education.* Monterey: Brooks/Cole.

Erikson, E.H. (1980) *Identity and the Life Cycle: A Reissue.* New York: W.W. Norton.

Garfield, S.L. and Bergin, A.E. (1986) *Handbook of Psychotherapy and Behaviour Change.* New York: Wiley.

Gilmore, S.K. (1973) *The Counselor-in-Training.* Englewood Cliffs, NJ: Prentice-Hall.

Gilmore, S.K. (1984) *Social and Communication Skills.* London: Unpublished lecture.

Grow, G.O. (1991) Teaching Learners to be Self-Directed: *Adult Education Quarterly* **41**(3), 125–149.

Hamblin, D. (1974) *The Teacher and Counselling*. Oxford: Basil Blackwell.

Handy, C. (1994) *The Empty Raincoat*. London: Hutchinson.

Hemming, J. (1977) Personal Development through Education. In J.B. Annand (ed.), *Education for Self-Discovery*. London: Hodder and Stoughton.

Heron, J. (1990) *Helping the Client*. London: Sage.

Hobbs, T. (ed.) (1992) *Experiential Training*. London: Tavistock/Routledge.

Holmes, J. and Lindley, R. (1991) *The Values of Psychotherapy*. Oxford: Oxford University Press.

Honey, P. and Mumford, A. (1986) *The Manual of Learning Styles*. Maidenhead: Honey & Murnford.

Houston, G. (1990) *The Red Book of Groups*. London: The Rochester Foundation.

Inskipp, F. (1993) *Counselling: The Trainers Handbook*. Cambridge: N.E.C.

Inskipp, F. (1996) *Skills Training for Counselling*. London: Cassell.

Irving, J.A. and Williams, D.I. (1995) Experience of Group Work in counsellor training and preferred learning styles. *Counselling Quarterly* 8(2), 139–144.

Jacobs, M. (1988) *Psychodynamic Counselling in Action*. London: Sage.

Jersild, A.T. (1955) *When Teachers Face Themselves*. New York: Teachers College Press.

Jourard, S.M. (1964) *The Transparent Self*. Princeton, NJ: Van Nostrand.

Kagan, N. (1967) *Studies in Human Interaction: Interpersonal Process Recall Stimulated by Videotape*. Michigan: Education Publications.

Kelly, G.A. (1955) *The Psychology of Personal Constructs 1 and 2*. New York: Norton.

Knights, B. (1995) *The Listening Reader*. London: Jessica Kingsley.

Kolb, D.A. (1984) *Experiential Learning*. London: Prentice-Hall.

Kurtz, R.R. (1975) *Structured Experiences in Groups*. Iowa: Annual Handbook for Group Facilitators.

Levine, B. (1980) Co-leadership Approaches to Learning Groupwork. *Social Work with Groups* 3(4), 38.

Mair, M. (1989) *Between Psychology and Psychotherapy: A Poetics of Experience*. London: Routledge.

Maslow, A.H. (1970, Third edition) *Motivation and Personality*. New York: Harper and Row.

McLeod, J. (1993) *An Introduction to Counselling*. Buckingham: Open University Press.

Mearns, D. (1994) *Developing Person-Centred Counselling*. London: Sage.

Mearns, D. and Thorne, B. (1988) *Person-Centred Counselling in Action*. London: Sage.

Miller, S., Nunnally, E.W. and Wackman, D.B. (1975) *Alive and Aware*. Minneapolis: Interpersonal Communication Programs, Inc.

Milner, M. (as Field, J.) (1934) *A Life of One's Own*. London: Chatto & Windus.

Mitchell, S. (1991). In G. Johnson and R. Kurtz, *Grace Unfolding*. New York: Bell Tower.

Morris, B. (1977) New Horizons and Lost Horizons: The Role of Feeling in Education. In J.B. Annand (ed.), *Education for Self-Discovery*. London: Hodder and Stoughton.

Murdoch, I. (1983) *Profile*. London: *The Times*, 15 April.

National Vocational Qualifications (1995) *First Release of Standards*. London: Lead Body for Advice, Guidance, Counselling and Psychotherapy.

Nelson-Jones, R. (1982) *The Theory and Practice of Counselling Psychology*. London: Holt, Rinehart and Winston.

Nelson-Jones, R. (1984) *Personal Responsibility Counselling and Therapy: An Integrative Approach*. London: Harper and Row.

Nye, R.D. (1986 Third edition) *Three Psychologies*. Monterey: Brooks/Cole.

Oatley, K. (1984) *Selves in Relation*. London: Methuen.

Patterson, C.H. (1986, Fourth edition) *Theories of Counselling and Psychotherapy*. New York: Harper and Row.

Proctor, B. (1978) *Counselling Shop*. London: Burnett Books/Andre Deutsch.

Proctor, B. (1991) On Being a Trainer. In W. Dryden and B. Thorne (eds), *Training and Supervision for Counselling in Action*. London: Sage.

Progoff, I. (1975) *At a Journal Workshop*. New York: Dialogue House Library.

Rainer, T. (1980) *The New Diary*. London: Angus and Robertston.

Robinson, W.L. (1974) Conscious Competency – the mark of a competent instructor. *Personnel Journal* 53, 538–539.

Rogers, A. (1986) *Teaching Adults*. Milton Keynes: Open University Press.

Rogers, C.R. (1961) *On Becoming a Person*. London: Constable.

Rogers, C.R. (1963) The Concept of the Fully-Functioning Person. *Psychotherapy: Theory, Research and Practice* 1(1), 17–26.

Rogers, C.R. (1978) *On Personal Power*. London: Constable.

Rogers, C.R. (1983) *Freedom to Learn for the 80's*. Columbus: Charles E Merrill.

Rowan, J. (1990) *Subpersonalities: The People Inside Us*. London: Routledge.

Rowan, J. (1995) What is Counselling About? A comparison of Four Positions in Personal Development. *Counselling* 6(2), 12–13.

Sartre, J.P. (1934). In G. Corey (1990) *Theory and Practice of Psychotherapy*. New York: Brooks/Cole.

Satir, V. (1972) *Peoplemaking*. London: Souvenir Press.

Satir, V. (1978) *Your Many Faces*. Berkeley: Celestial Arts.

Smith, P.B. (1980) *Group Processes and Personal Change*. London: Harper and Row.

Socrates (469–399BC) In J. Urmson and P. Ree, *Encyclopaedia of Western Philosophy and Philosophers*. London: Unwin Heinemann.

Speedy, J. (1993) *Heroines, Healers, Harlots, and Hags*. Unpublished MSc Thesis: University of Bristol.

Stedeford, A. (1989) Counselling, Death and Bereavement. In W. Dryden, D. Charles-Edwards and R. Woolfe (eds) *Handbook of Counselling in Britain*. London: Tavistock/Routledge.

Strong, S.R. (1968) Counseling: An interpersonal influence process. *Journal of Counseling Psychology* 15, 215–224.

Sugarman, L. (1986) *Life-Span Development*. London: Methuen.

Thorne, B. (1987) Beyond the Core Conditions. In W. Dryden (ed.) *Key Cases in Psychotherapy*. London: Croom Helm.

Tight, M. (1983) *Education for Adults*. London: Croom Helm/Open University.

Tough, A. (1976) Self-planned Learning and Major Personal Change. In R.M. Smith (ed.) *Adult Learning: Issues and Innovations.* Northern Illinois: ERIC.

Trower, P., Casey, A. and Dryden, W. (1988) *Cognitive-Behavioural Counselling in Action.* London: Sage.

van Deurzen-Smith, E. (1988) *Existential Counselling in Practice.* London: Sage.

van Deurzen-Smith (1992). In W. Dryden (ed.) *Hard-Earned Lessons from Counselling in Action.* London: Sage.

van Deurzen-Smith (1993) Changing the World: Possibilities and Limitations. *Counselling* 4(2), 120–123.

Velleman, R. (1989) Counselling people with alcohol and drug problems. In W. Dryden, D. Charles-Edwards and R. Woolfe (eds) *Handbook of Counselling in Britain.* London: Tavistock/Routledge.

Vernelle, B. (1994) *Understanding and Using Groups.* London: Whiting and Birch Ltd.

Wall, W.D. (1977) The Search for Identity. In J.B. Annand (ed.), *Education for Self-Discovery.* London: Hodder and Stoughton.

Whiteley, J.M., Sprinthall, N.A., Mosher, R.L. and Donaghy, R.T. (1967) Selection and Evaluation of Counselor Effectiveness. *Journal of Counselling Psychology*, **14**, 226–234.

Whitmore, D. (1991) *Psychosynthesis Counselling in Action.* London: Sage.

Wilberg, K. (1990) Two Patterns of Transcendance: A reply to Washburn. *Journal of Humanistic Psychology*, **30**(3), 113–136.

Winnicott, D.W. (1971) *Playing and Reality.* London: Hogarth.

Wolinsky, S. (1994) *The Tao of Chaos: Essence and the Enneagram.* Connecticut: Bramble Books.

Woolfe, R. and Sugarman, L. (1989) Counselling and the Life Cycle. In W. Dryden, D. Charles-Edwards and R. Woolfe (eds) *Handbook of Counselling in Britain.* London: Tavistock/Routledge.

Name Index

Subject Index